Creativity and Culture
Art Projects
for Primary Schools

REFERENCE

ONLY

Creativity and Culture
Art Projects
for Primary Schools

Nigel Meager

nsead Publications

Published by the National Society for Education
in Art and Design in 2006

NSEAD
The Gatehouse
Corsham Court
Corsham
Wiltshire SN13 OBZ
United Kingdom
Tel: +44 (0) 1249 714825
Fax: +44 (0) 1249 716138

www.nsead.org

© Nigel Meager, 2006

British Library Cataloguing in Publication Data

A CIP record for this book is available from the
British Library.

ISBN 0 904684 30 X

Designed by SteersMcgillan Design Limited

www.steersmcgillan.co.uk

Printed by Studio Fasoli, Verona, Italy

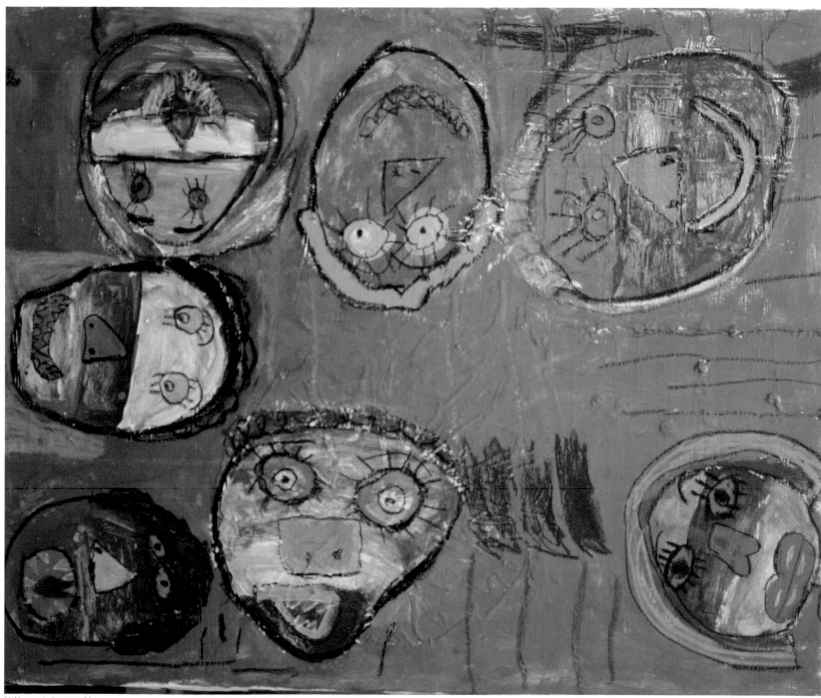

Making portraits, page 80

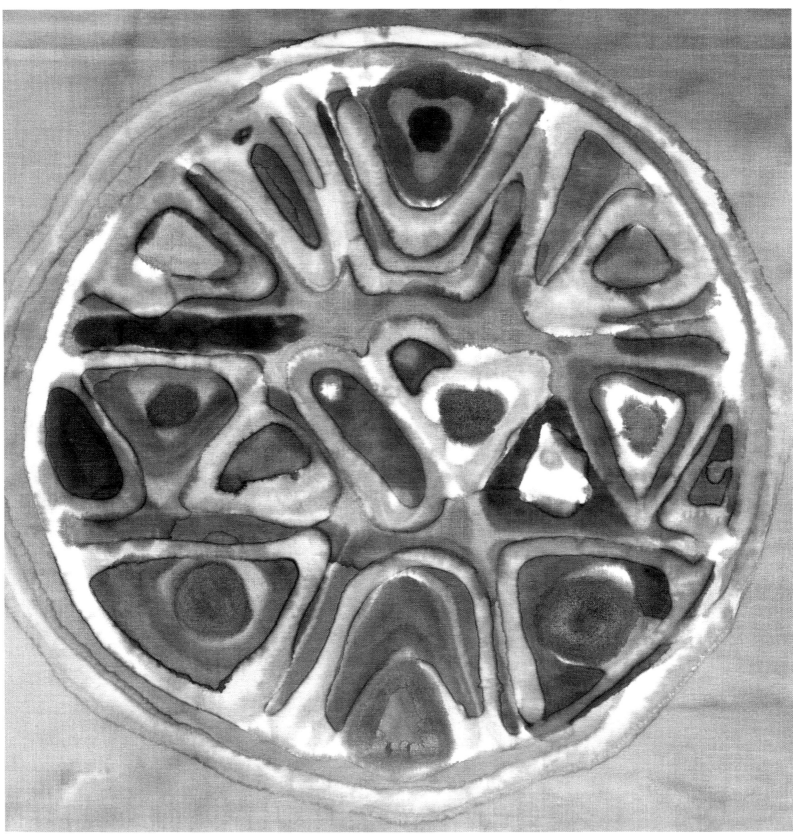

Paste resist, page 58

Background

This book describes ideas about teaching art in primary schools. The author, Nigel Meager, has worked as a freelance art educator in the United Kingdom since 1987. The focus of his work has been in primary schools or working with local authorities delivering in-service training for teachers. In the early 1990s Nigel concluded his work on the Visual Impact Project, a long-term artist in residency project in West Glamorgan funded by the Gulbenkian Foundation and others. The outcome was 'Teaching Art at Key Stage 1', written for infant school teachers working with children from 3 to 7 years of age and published by the National Society for Education in Art and Design (NSEAD) in 1993. TAKS1 was followed by 'Teaching Art at Key Stage 2', for teachers of children 7 to 11 years of age (co-authored with Julie Ashfield) and again published by NSEAD in 1995. Both books described, in detail, art projects for the classroom aimed at helping teachers with no specialist art training. 'Teaching Art at Key Stage 1' promised that, 'You don't need to be good at art to teach it well'.

'TAKS1' and 'TAKS2' had at their core the idea that it is possible to demystify art by breaking down some of the important concepts and practices into small and easy to understand portions, which are then built one upon another to create a richer experience for children. The concepts included the visual elements of colour, tone, pattern, form, space, texture, shape and line. The practices included painting, drawing, collage, working with clay, sculptural construction and printing. Advice about introducing examples of adult art to children was integrated into the project structures. The teaching strategies placed an emphasis on talking and the kind of language that teachers can use to help children understand key concepts and learn basic skills. The books were a considerable success and are still in print over ten years after their first appearances.

The ideas in TAKS1 and TAKS2 resonated with the content of the early versions of the National Curriculum for Art in both England and Wales (and perhaps to a lesser extent Scotland and Northern Ireland). The English curriculum, for example, was structured under the two Attainment Target headings of 'Investigating and Making' and 'Knowledge and Understanding'. The ideas seemed to suggest that the twin approaches of investigating the world and discovering adult art would inspire and give meaning to children's art. The curriculum also provided a clear structure of ideas from which planning, in the form of schemes and units of work, could be structured.

In 2001 Nigel Meager was invited by advisors for Cardiff schools to contribute to what became an ongoing series of teacher training workshops, first devoted to Early Years teachers and later for teachers at Key Stages 1 and 2. The initial inspiration was the work of educators in Reggio Emilia in Italy who have pioneered ways of placing ideas created by the child (rather than ideas prescribed by the teacher) at the centre of how projects are planned and implemented. The key emphasis is always on creativity. However, Cardiff is not in Italy, and so ways of working were designed that took essential ideas about creativity but made sure that these fitted with the best of what teachers were already doing in Cardiff schools and were practical in the context of available funding and resources. The Early Years workshops went well so the team, that included Nigel Meager, Julie Ashfield, Robert Cornelius and Chris Glynn, explored how similar ways of working could be developed for all children in primary school. These projects showed how teachers could design art projects that allowed children to create and control the meaning of their art work, whilst at the same time benefiting from a supportive and directed teacher controlled precinct of ideas.

The Cardiff initiative was the springboard for the development of the ideas described in this book. It swiftly became apparent that the same teaching strategies that helped children create meaning could also lead to children creating something that looked like imaginary, embryonic cultures. The evidence suggested that as children's ideas were layered one on another, they became increasingly diverse so that groups within the same class, working within the same teacher directed environments, could produce very different outcomes. The creation of these imaginary cultures also seemed to facilitate children's understanding of art from other cultures. In other words, having gone through the process of creating their own art with cultural meaning and expression, children could more readily grasp that other art objects created by other people would have similar meanings too.

The bottom line was whether the kinds of teaching strategies that are now described in this book really could help to inspire and motivate teachers and children? Were the three threads of creativity, culture and meaning able to be woven into realistic classroom-based activities? Did teaching of the arts benefit in general? Was the potential for learning enhanced? The answer to all four questions seemed to be yes. Could these ideas be described in a way that teachers with no special training in the arts could put them into practice in the classroom? This was the challenge that led to this publication.

Much work was organised with children to help trial and develop these kinds of projects. Lessons were learnt and strategies improved as a result of classroom experience. The flagship project revolved around creating an imaginary island. In the summer of 2005, Cardiff organised an extensive programme to promote the imaginary island project and the underlying principles of this way of working in schools. Head teachers, deputy head teachers, classroom teachers, children and a team of artists from different arts disciplines contributed to a series of events including training, lectures, conferences and workshops. The initiative was called 'Islands of Imagination'.

Acknowledgements

The author would like to thank the following people:

Dr. John Steers from the National Society for Education in Art & Design whose advice and encouragement has been so important from the very first discussion of this project. Julie Ashfield and Robert Cornelius from Cardiff LEA for their unstinting support and openness to try new ideas. Professor Nick Stanley for reading and commenting on the draft copies. Artist, designer and musician, Chris Glynn, for his expansive creativity and the map of Illuzia. Teachers and children in the following Cardiff, Swansea and Rhondda/Cynon/Taff schools:

Bishop Childs, Christ the King, Cila, Clase, Coed Glas, Cwmlai, Gladstone, Glan-Yr-Afon, Glyncollen, Holy Family, Knelston, Llandaff C.W., Llwynderw, Llanishen Fach, Llysfaen, Mayals, Meadowbank, St Bernadette's, St Helens, St John Lloyd, St Joseph's, St Peter's, St Phillip Evans, St Thomas, Thornhill, Tremorfa, Trowbridge Junior, Waun Wen, Willowbrook, Ysgol y Berllen Deg, Ysgol Bro Eirwg.

Children from these schools worked on at least one of the projects described in this book. A special mention to the 2003–2005 Year 5 and 6 class of Knelston Primary School, Swansea – thank you for your creativity, intelligence and good humour.

Finally thanks to the skill and vision of designers Richard McGillan, Leon White and Ian Stratford of SteersMcGillan Design Limited, indexer Susan Vaughan and two contemporary art galleries: Mission Gallery, Swansea (Jane Phillips and Amanda Roderick) and BayArt Cardiff, (Phil Nichol and Maggie James).

Photography:
Nigel Meager, Roy Campbell-Moore, Geraldine Deayton and Julie Ashfield.

Contents

Part 1
Creating cultures

When you see this symbol (»146) in the text it refers to further information that can be found on the indicated page in the Appendix.

Preface

In recent years the education pendulum once again has swung decisively towards recognising the importance of creativity in education. At the same time the ability to motivate pupils effectively more often continues to be regarded as the fortunate gift of the talented teacher rather than something that can be consciously nurtured as part of any well considered pedagogy. If we wish to firmly establish a central role for creativity in schools then providing proper opportunities, a supportive environment and keen motivation will be crucial. This is exactly what artist-educator Nigel Meager seeks to promote in this book.

Creativity is not rare in the sense that the ability to be creative or to think creatively is not limited to those who gain recognition as creative geniuses. On one level, creativity is a commonplace human attribute: most people solve problems creatively quite regularly – at work, at home, at school, in the garden, wherever… I find it most useful to think of 'creativity' as shorthand for a raft of multi-faceted abilities and predispositions that should be fostered throughout the curriculum. Creative individuals, including creative children in the primary school classroom, may display a wide range of characteristics but these might include: a tolerance for ambiguity and a willing playfulness with ideas, materials or processes; an ability to concentrate and persist, to keep on teasing and worrying away at an idea or problem rather than seeking premature closure. (Creativity cannot be rushed or reduced to a formula: there is often an incubation period before creative ideas may occasionally gel in that elusive 'Eureka!' moment.) They are people who are likely to recognise, or have a readiness to explore, unlikely connections, juxtapositions. They may be particularly

self-aware and sometimes have the courage (or stubbornness) to pursue their ideas in the face of opposition. Most of all, creative individuals must have the confidence, the self-belief to take intellectual and intuitive risks in the cause of innovation, and as adults, breaking or pushing back the boundaries of what is known or thought possible. Perhaps the definition I like best is that, quite simply, creativity is 'risky thinking'.

Four phases of the creative process have been identified. First there is *Preparation* in which the problem or question is defined, reformulated and redefined. Second, there is *Generation* – moving beyond habitual pathways of thinking. Third, there is an *Incubation* period – conscious planning and subconscious scanning of the problem or idea often following a period of relaxed attention. Finally *Verification* where ideas are analysed, synthesised and evaluated, followed by detailed planning and implementation. It is important to stress that the process is rarely straightforward and usually there is interplay between these elements, with various phases being revisited and reviewed – for example when dead ends seem apparent. This suggests that providing adequate time or 'creative space' is a crucial requirement if the creative spark is to flourish. There are other necessary preconditions that are equally important for both teachers and children: developing an atmosphere of mutual trust and affective support; the constructive use of probing questioning to increase the intellectual challenge; allowing children to develop a real sense of ownership of the task or problem; and bolstering confidence and self-esteem.

It is soon apparent that promoting creativity or 'risky thinking' may not always sit easily alongside the everyday classroom pressures and controlled prescriptions of national curricula, literacy and

numeracy hours, assessment and inspection. In many schools the prevalent view is that it is best to play safe, to stick to the established routines and not to take any chances. But creative children need creative teachers with the confidence to take creative risks.

Perceived intelligence and creativity are not necessarily closely correlated. E P Torrance, writing over thirty years ago, pointed out that '…if we were to identify children as gifted on the basis of intelligence tests, we would eliminate from consideration approximately seventy per cent of the most creative'.[1] He also observed that teachers tend to rate more highly the children with high IQs on most counts but he noted that highly creative children appear to learn as much as the highly intelligent without seeming to work as hard. Why? He concluded that highly creative children are often learning and thinking when they appear to be just 'playing around'. Might such creative individuals often seem difficult to manage in the classroom situation, because they often want to follow their own agendas, at their own pace, rather than that of the teacher? What happens to their potential creativity as a consequence?

Motivation is an internal state – a need or desire – that serves to activate or energise behaviour and give it direction. Of course, incentives such as receiving privileges and praise can motivate learning. However if motivation is to be *intrinsic*, rather than *extrinsic* and ephemeral, interest and effort should be encouraged through strategies that encourage self-sufficient learning, provide children with an element of choice, with control over challenge and opportunities to work collaboratively. Teacher response has an important role in determining further learning: children are influenced by feedback from earlier performance on similar tasks especially in relation to the *effort* they invest in further work. Such feedback needs to bolster confidence rather than simply focus on the shortcomings of completed tasks. Positive inter-personal relationships between teachers and children matter very much: constructive discussion to create an ethos that supports children's feelings of self-worth and effort is vital. Education systems that place undue emphasis on evaluation tend to produce children with strong extrinsic orientation towards grades and social status rather than supporting deeper learning.

Encouraging determination and persistence are also keys to maintaining effective motivation. It is self-evident that success is predictably more motivating than failure. Therefore, '...if an individual doesn't believe he or she can be successful at a task *or* the individual does not see a connection between his or her activity and success *or* the individual does not value the results of success, then the probability is lowered that the individual will engage in the required learning activity'.[2]

It is worth remembering that developing extrinsic motivation – for example, by means of overt reward and punishment – may work in the classroom for a time but usually only while children are under the teacher's direct control. Teaching that too directly addresses pre-determined assessment criteria, standards and targets too often inhibits real creativity and motivation. Teachers, and even artists working in schools, can all too often seek to control the outcomes to such an extent that ownership of the meaning of their work is taken away from the children. So the following suggestions, which are at the core of this book, are aimed primarily at developing lasting intrinsic motivation and creative capacity:

- *Planning the learning experience* with care to arouse and maintain children's curiosity; offering a clear and supportive framework for learning while avoiding prescriptions that would determine outcomes.
- *Providing opportunities for discussions* which attract attention to the complexity of art, culture and how we live together in society, thereby, arousing interest; avoiding repetition and orthodoxy by seeking varied teaching strategies and content; organising a variety of activities that involve play, surprise, and ingenuity; explaining or demonstrating why learning about particular contexts or skills is important.
- *Empathy for your children's aptitudes* for art and what is meaningful to them; finding ways to channel their interests and the issues that concern them into worthwhile objectives and art projects; and allowing them to proceed at a pace commensurate with their ability and effective individual and collaborative patterns of working.
- *Offering feedback* that boosts children's self-esteem through appreciative critiques rather than just corrective criticism. Listening to children's own assessments of what they have achieved and encouraging them to learn from each other; helping them evaluate their progress and the outcomes of their work, thus providing a stimulus for further accomplishments.

Finally remember 'Creativity is not only an outcome of a good education, but a means of achieving a good education'.[3]

John Steers
General Secretary, National Society for Education in Art & Design

Notes
1 Torrance, E (1970) 'Stimulating Creativity', in Vernon, P (ed), Creativity, Penguin Books, Harmondsworth, p.358.
2 Huitt, W (2001) 'Motivation to learn: An overview', Educational Psychology Interactive, Valdosta GA: Valdosta State University. Retrieved 23rd September 2004 from http://chiron.valdosta.edu/whuitt/col/motivation/motivate.html
3 Attributed to Sir Michael Barber, former head of the DfES Standards and Effectiveness Unit.

Introduction

Orientation

This book contains descriptions of classroom projects for primary schools. These are written for teachers and student teachers who have no special training or experience in the arts and who do not normally have special access to external human resources, such as visiting artists, or art education specialists. There are examples of teaching strategies that enable children to be creative and to find and express their own meanings. The projects, many of which are described in detail, also open opportunities for children to understand more about how people come to together to create culture and society.

The introduction considers the elusive concepts of culture and creativity and so offers an insight into the thinking behind the work in the classroom. It discusses the difficulty of ascribing absolute values to arts education. It wonders whether it is better to fit the curriculum to the practice rather than the practice to the curriculum. The intention is to reflect the real richness and diversity of arts practice (echoing the richness and diversity of cultural life) and so celebrate the endless possibilities for teachers and children to find and create the new. This contrasts with linear and hierarchical curriculum planning structures.

Inevitably, there is a sense of shifting ground and swirling movement through ideas. Although it is difficult to feel secure without the certainty of overarching curricula and hierarchical planning structures, if the teacher looks carefully and in detail at the examples of arts projects and practices in this book, she may see that they are not difficult to teach. Just like the individual skeletal components of coral, the projects are both structurally sound and well formed in detail. Like coral, they build one on another, but in endlessly varying ways. So each unique classroom project will contribute to a rich arts experience for children and help them to understand how their own creativity functions and how cultures are formed, from wherever and from whomsoever.

The section 'ideas about how to use this book' offers guidance about how teachers may get the most out of the projects described. This section links to established primary art education concepts such as investigation, the visual elements and teaching skills. There is the first mention of a strategy that teachers could use to plan projects that have ideas at their centre.

It is hoped that the reader can dip in and out of this book. Getting to know an approach such as this is like getting to know a person. It is true that first impressions are important but equally, the more familiar and at ease you become, the more interesting and multi-layered is the character that emerges. It is also true that hearing about the background to a person may not be very interesting unless you know that person first. So, if you skip this introduction to get to know the body of the book, why not come back later – especially if you discover you are beginning to like what you find and want to know more?

Using pattern, page 37

Culture and cultural relativism

Talking generally about arts education and more specifically about its practice in classrooms, necessarily involves the use of words that define concepts and ideas. The relationship between what we see and experience, what we want to see and experience and these concepts and the words that stand for them is mobile and puzzling. In this sense, the concepts *culture* and *creativity* are difficult to pin down; if it is indeed the 'pinning down' that we think will be valuable.

A comprehensive understanding of culture goes far beyond the scope of this introduction. However, it may be valuable to briefly note uses of the concept and how these interplay with the belief that building cultural awareness is an important, perhaps essential, educational objective in the primary classroom. In the most sweepingly wide terms, culture could be seen as 'the ensemble of stories we tell ourselves about ourselves'[1] or to say the same thing another way, 'the ways we describe what we are'. The word and concept of culture are everywhere, its use is ubiquitous. Culture can be an indiscriminate word, bandied about in the popular media and friendly discussions. Nevertheless, it does seem to have some moral or even aesthetic force; we do sense what it means in a plethora of different contexts. We can talk about popular culture, high culture, business culture, street culture, urban culture, folk culture, playground culture, global culture, national culture, multiculturalism, the cultural divide and cultural values. We can become cultivated. In the post-modern world, cultures can be ripped out of their normal geographical context as people move freely from country to country and continent to continent. Cultures can be mixed up together, becoming indecipherable as separate entities. Some older cultures survive but become mutated. More than ever, cultural identities are hybridised and carried all over the world by electronic media.

Closer to home, our culture is a part of our identity. How we behave, what we believe, the decisions we take and the lives we lead, reflect the culture we were born into, the cultures that influence us as we grow up and the cultures we form part of as adults. Each primary school has its own cultural identity. There may be a uniform, a school colour. A school may be well known for its friendliness, ability at team sports, its musical performances or the caring politeness of its children. Although to an outsider, the inside of one primary school might look very much like the inside of another, as primary schools share features (classrooms, the curriculum, display boards, playgrounds, lunch times) which mean they have very similar cultures. It depends on your point of view.

The culture industry is a dominant influence in the lives of both children and adults. We watch television, we listen to popular music, we enjoy cinema both on the big screen and on DVD. Toys, clothes, branded goods of all kinds are commercial spin offs from mass media, entertainment and sport. Huge companies are formed to both create and distribute mass culture in order to make profit for their shareholders. Here, in the guise of entertainment, cultural norms, values, beliefs and behaviours are in endless and confusing flux. In the past two days the author, as he writes the first draft of this introduction, has watched an episode from 'The Shield', an amoral, violent and disturbing police drama based in Los Angeles whose central character, Vic Mackey, is a detective who through his corruption and his ability to enter into the culture of drug crime is able to manage and control the worst excesses of the violent street. He has watched 'Finding Nemo', a Disney production, in which some critics say the saccharin values of the protected white middle class in the USA are ascribed to cartoon fish. He has listened to 'Buena Vista Social Club', a Cuban salsa inspired ensemble much admired by an icon of western jazz, Ry Cooder, who argues that this 'refined and deeply funky music is made in an atmosphere sealed off from the fall out of a hyper-organised and noisy world. He has read part of 'Cosmic Banditos' a comic novel, written by a surfer now living in a remote corner of Costa Rica, which is about a down-on-his-luck pot smuggler who discovers that the absurdities implied in quantum mechanics mirror life; and he has also read extracts from the Oxford Book of Dreams. On top of this, there have been television and radio news reports about men in black tights and the invasion of the British parliament by aficionados of fox hunting, watched, it has to be admitted, as much for entertainment as information. The point here is not to give you, the reader, a disturbing insight in to the author's mind, but on what have been really two quite ordinary days, to show the overwhelming, drenching, drowning, swirling flood of products from the culture industry. One could spend years analysing the meanings of the TV drama, film, news reports, music and books just mentioned. They probably contain a fair cross section of the norms, values and behaviours of our broader western culture. They certainly illustrate that without moving very far (out of the house in this case) one has easy access to the culture of many, many different groups and sub-groups in societies. Do we need to make sense of it at all? Have we an obligation to educate children to be aware of and prepared for this cultural mêlée and what it means?

Designing a motif, page 35

Society, and the smaller ever shifting groupings that form it, comprise not an amorphous lump but a complex, interrelated and therefore amazingly rich and diverse cultural environment. This became a widely accepted view in the latter half of the twentieth century. I cannot express this better than Marsh and Millard who write that culture exists both in and outside the individual as a complex pattern of meanings expressed in a variety of ways. Culture is constructed by groups as they share discourse. We are born into a set of cultural values and norms and acquire others through cultural interaction. The elitism implied by concepts of high culture has been largely left behind. The vision of culture is now more than just the best that has been thought and known, it also celebrates the complexity of an individual's cultural identity made up of so many meanings from so many different sources. This plurality cannot be easily simplified or categorised.[2]

The role of other cultures or different cultures has had a powerful impact on art and design education in recent years. Teachers have been advised on training courses to research and resource examples of visual art from a range of different cultures, from different times in history and different parts of the world. These could be integrated into projects. Here are two typical examples. Children might be taught to mix colours. A reproduction of a landscape painting from nineteenth century France is divided into small rectangles. Each child is given a rectangle and asked to copy the colours she finds. The children's painted rectangles are then reassembled and compared to the original reproduction. They have been introduced to a different culture that in this case features ideas about representing landscape in nineteenth century France. Or children are shown examples of pattern

from Islamic buildings. They make copies in their sketchbooks. They go on to make clay tiles and use elements from the patterns in their sketchbooks to decorate their tiles. They have been introduced to Islamic art. Boxes are ticked. In each of these examples, children have learnt skills, but have they learnt anything about culture? In the context of the pluralistic view of culture that has already been described, it is worth trying to unpick one of the key aims of this book: to help teachers help children achieve a heightened cultural awareness and understanding.

The teacher designs arts projects that have skeletal structures that focus on helping children create their own meanings as they work, both individually and within a group, communicating ideas. These projects are useful as they show how patterns of meaning are created collectively by the group and how the individual finds his or her own personal expressive forms within this shared structure. Groups and individuals create collective representations of meaning, which are formalised in a symbolic way. These representations might be songs, a dance, costumes, stories, poems, paintings, drawings, printed fabrics, digital photographs and much else besides. In this process small imaginary cultures are created (or highlighted) within which, the child can sense that their own expression makes sense and has a place. The group goes on to establish these 'stories that we tell ourselves about ourselves' in different art forms. The norms, meanings and values present in their work are shared through interaction. The interaction happens as the child works as part of (or at the very least alongside) the class or a group, as they develop ideas, and as they perform or show their ideas to others. The children will have experienced the

formation of an imaginary culture (a pattern of meanings embodied in symbolic forms which exist both inside and outside the individual). This is very exciting for a child and mirrors in the more formal setting of the classroom the kinds of imaginary interactions that they may establish through play. Because children create the meanings (the content was not dictated or overly controlled by the adult), their work means a lot to them.

As they take part in such projects, such as those in this book, children become used to the idea that groups of people create culture based on shared meanings. The opportunity now exists to introduce children to expressions of other cultures in terms of what those expressions mean to the societies, groups and individuals who made them, rather than the simple gloss of how they look. Children will also see that the 'where' and the 'what' of how life is led also influences cultural outcomes. So, for example, look at page 38 and the examples of weaving from a Guatemalan village. Because children created their own patterns as part of a project built around imaginary communities, they were fascinated to learn that the patterns and motifs made by the Guatemalan weavers carried meanings. The Guatemalan villagers have their own culture, which in part, reflected their geography, mythology, economic circumstance and family traditions. Children understood more about this because they had already experienced a process through which, they had created cultural meanings of their own. The plurality of cultural expressions that are consumed or created by children inside and outside the classroom cannot be easily simplified or categorised, they are as multifarious, multi-dimensional and as complex as the bio-diverse environment of a rainforest or as the structural wonders of the miniature creatures that in their millions combine to form coral reefs. Although this book does not attempt to describe a specific curriculum model, perhaps these two examples of eco systems provide better examples of what the structure of a culturally balanced arts curriculum might look like than the some of the more linear and hierarchical models of recent times.

Cultural relativism

However, before we look at our second key concept, *creativity*, in more detail, consider the potentially puzzlingly culturally relative state of art education itself and the terms and concepts it subsumes. All descriptions, analyses, theories, programmes and projects in arts education are in part and by their nature, culturally relative to their time and place. That is, it is difficult to assign absolute values to arts education as though we were able to define an absolute cultural standard. Something like a definite cultural standard, overarching time and place, would mean that the art curriculum would be likely to be finite and unchallengeable, we would be certain about our goals and staunch in their defence. However, from time to time, concepts and ways of working emerge with properties that can seem to be almost as powerful as absolute standards. During the late twentieth century, in primary school visual arts education in the United Kingdom, we could track the emergence of buzz words and phrases such as *learning skills, observation, critical studies, metamorphosis, investigating and making, other cultures, the visual elements, working with artists* and most recently (in the early part of the first decade of the twenty first century) *creativity* and *information technology*. Concepts like these galvanise art educators, teacher trainers and art advisors who programme training

courses, devise strategies and go on to excite teachers who, in turn, enthusiastically put the ideas into practice in the classroom. Books, documents and schemes of work are written that describe structures of ideas that seem implacably correct. That is, they must be followed. But if we accept that intrinsic to the nature of the arts, are characteristics such as pluralism, ambiguity, serendipity, imagination, individuality, creativity, and so forth, then attempts to define art education practice in just one kind of mega-theory or super-curriculum are curiously futile. So why do we keep trying? Partly to protect the integrity of the subject, because if the arts in schools cannot be described in the same kinds of models as other subjects then they might be seen by civil servants, politicians and even education opinion formers as somehow lesser; partly to help teachers who must teach art to children in busy crowded classrooms, who in primary schools are not art specialists, who have had limited training in teaching the arts and who simply need support; and partly because it is so difficult to work in unstructured ways faced with the huge and wondrous jungle of art practice. Simple structures and definitive models obviously are going to be helpful to some teachers and student teachers who self effacingly admit that they do not really understand the arts or how to teach them. Progress is made. The arts are taught. Children create and are proud of their work.

It is hoped that this book describes ideas about teaching art in primary school in a clear and simple way. A way that results in classroom practices that are genuinely accessible to non-arts specialist primary school teachers, that is not hierarchical and overarching, is respectful of its culturally relative place and is receptive to characteristics such as pluralism, ambiguity, serendipity, imagination, individuality and creativity.

So there are no overt hierarchical curriculum planning structures to be found here. If you are not too confident about teaching art, then the ground may begin to feel unsure but, perhaps, a little more real. To increase the sense of an absence of certainty, consider the many different readings that will be possible depending on the circumstances of you, the reader. You may be a student teacher in the first year of training needing to complete an assignment, a classroom teacher looking for help in planning lessons, an experienced (or inexperienced) art coordinator responsible for planning art in your school, a head teacher, a lecturer in education or art education, an art advisor or advisory teacher, an artist who works in schools, a freelance educator who devises and coordinates projects, a gallery educator, a civil servant, an academic. Also you may be reading this shortly after its publication (in which case it may feel new); you may be eagerly looking for practical support for a classroom art project next school year and already wanting to flip ahead to the projects themselves; or you may be a reader some forty years hence who has found this book in an odd corner of an on-line book store and is curious about some of the patterns of ideas in primary art education current in the first ten years of the twenty-first century. You may be from the United Kingdom where the author works (and if you live in Glasgow your points of reference on the contents will not be the same as if you live in Cardiff), or perhaps you live in the USA or New Zealand, Japan, India or Costa Rica.

The point of such ramblings is to describe how the ideas already described and those that follow, are ebbing, flowing, turning, twisting in cultural currents that are already way out of reach of the control of the reader, author or the publisher. In the classroom, if the

Notes

1 Clifford Geertze, *The interpretation of Cultures*, London: Hutchinson (1975), pp 444-5 this definition is valued and quoted several times in a useful introduction to culture: Fred Inglis, *Culture*, Cambridge: Polity Press (2004).
2 Paraphrased from Jackie Marsh and Elaine Millard, *Literacy and Popular Culture*: London, Paul Chapman Educational Publishing (2001), p15.

Dream collage, page 104

teacher can feel the confidence in herself to let go of the children's ideas and allow their thoughts and expressions to flow or move more freely, then these ideas will be, in one important sense, out of her control. This means they are more likely to belong to the child because they have been freely created by that child. However, teachers must still be able to direct what and how the children are learning. Teachers will need to set boundaries and rules, precincts within which children work. The nature of classroom projects described here echo the same kind of precarious balances that are found in life between polarising ideas like prescription and liberty, (for example, in the balance between the control of the state and the freedom of the individual).

Finally, in the twenty years preceding 2005 and writing this passage, some theorists have even suggested that the boundaries between the fantasy cultures disseminated by the mass cultural industries and what would have once been called reality, have become so blurred that they merge into one. We live in the fantasies that the free market has created for us to consume. This market also makes us all wealthier as economies grow. Any notion of one culture for one society has disintegrated into countless tiny mini-cultures, which emerge, merge, separate, cross-refer, swirl and die. Local and traditional folk cultures are swept up in this confusion and lost. What is really my culture, or yours? Is it still possible to say? If children can experience creating their own imaginary cultures as part of art in primary school, they may be better able to find their feet in the growing cultural maelstrom of global living. This idea works because we are teaching children at a deeper level. They are learning about *how* culture works before we show them examples of *what* culture is.

Making portraits, page 80

Creativity

As we have seen, the term 'culture' can appear to be so wide a concept that it can all at once seem to mean both everything and nothing. In the other major theme of this book, the term 'creativity' is equally slippery. Clearly if a child, under the keen direction of a teacher, makes a painting then she is being to some extent creative. Something new is made. To help explain what this book attempts to do it is useful to think about the kinds of projects that are not included.

Consider the following three examples. An artist has developed a particular technique for painting sunsets. Her paintings are popular and sell well. As part of a programme to encourage creativity and direct experience of the arts, a school invites this artist to work with children. She asks that each child be given a set of poster colours that she has premixed herself. They are all given the same size of paper mounted on to board. Each child has the same three different sizes of brush. The children are sitting at tables all facing the artist who has placed her own empty paper on an easel so that all the children can see. She begins,

'First dip your largest brush into the water and then into purple blue colour. Make sure it goes all the way in so that you have a lot of colour on the brush. Take it out of the colour slowly and carefully and watch where I put my brush on the paper. Now you place your brush on your paper and follow me as I drag my brush to the right. Well done, you have made your first sunset mark. Now rinse the brush well in your water and wipe it with the rag. Now we can move on to the orange colour. Look carefully at where I put the orange on my painting and then try yourselves...'

For our second example, the teacher has read this author's 'Teaching Art at Key Stage 1'.[1] He is working with Year 4 pupils in an English primary school but is not at all sure if they have had much experience creating tone, one of the visual elements listed in the National Curriculum programme of study. He wants them to make portraits of each other using charcoal and chalk. He turns to page 64:

'Here is some charcoal and some chalk. Which one would you use to make a dark patch? Which one would you use to make a light patch? You can experiment and make dark and light patches on your paper. After you have finished I would like you to tell me what happens when you mix the charcoal and chalk together.'

The teacher hands each child a sheet of A2 grey sugar paper. Children cover the paper in patches of charcoal and chalk mixed together. The teacher hands out new sheets of A2 grey paper and asks the children to use masking tape to fix these onto drawing boards. The children pair off and each pair sits facing each other across the table. They place the drawing boards on their knees, leaning the board against the edge of the table.

The teacher says, 'Look at you partner's head, Where can you see the darkest parts of the head? Where can you see the lightest parts? Where can you see shadows? We have been experimenting with charcoal and chalk making light, dark and grey patches. When you draw look for the dark and light areas and look for shadows. Draw carefully and put in whatever you can see. Don't draw the outline first but pick a spot in the middle somewhere, start there and work towards the outside of the head. This means you will probably start with the eyes, the nose and the mouth. Keep going and don't worry about your mistakes.'

For our third example an artist visits a primary school to work with year six pupils, he is very familiar with the work of British artist, Richard Long[2]. Long makes sculptures by walking in landscapes and in some way changing elements of that landscape along the walk and recording what he has done, often taking photographs. Indeed the visiting artist's own work is greatly influenced by Long. He begins the day by showing children examples of Long's work in books and from the Internet. They project some images onto the whiteboard and the artist explains how Long set about making the work.

The artist shows children one example where Long has collected a great number of stones from a dry riverbed and bit by bit arranged them into a large spiral. He tells the children that they are going to take a coach down to a nearby beach and as the tide is out, they will be able to walk along the shoreline and collect pebbles, which they will use to make their own huge spiral on the sand. They will be using digital cameras to record the event.

The children are excited. They arrive at the beach and the artist suggests that the class splits into three. One third will collect dark pebbles, one third mid-coloured pebbles and the final third light coloured pebbles. There is a discussion about what to do. The artist marks the place on the sand where the spiral will start and the children begin their walk along the beach collecting stones. The artist and teacher take photos. After a while, the artist blows a whistle and the children return with their stones. The teacher organises the class so that one after another they place a light stone, then a mid coloured stone and then a dark coloured stone until they can see that the spiral is growing. The artist remains on hand to make sure that the spiral looks good and that the children

Notes

1 Published in 1993 by NSEAD.
2 Use the key words 'Richard Long' to search the internet to find out about the artist, his ideas and his work.
3 National Endowment for Science Technology and the Arts.
4 National Advisory Committee on Creative and Cultural Education (1999) *All our futures: Creativity, Culture and Education,* Sudbury, DfEE.
5 Dr John Steers, National Society for Education in Art and Design.
6 For example, Nigel Meager, Teaching Art at Key Stage 1, (1993), NSEAD, and by the same author and publisher, Teaching Art at Key Stage 2 (1995) and within the searchable units of work on the NSEAD web site, www.nsead.org. A number of skills are descibed in the appendix.

accurately place the stones. They continue until they have made a really big spiral. Photographs are taken and the children make drawings in their sketchbooks of the spiral using soft pencils. Whilst the children are enjoying a picnic lunch, the tide, gradually at first and then with some violence, destroys the spiral. The photographs, drawings, and examples of children writing about the day are displayed in school alongside reproductions of Richard Long's art. An art advisory teacher in the local authority uses the project as an example of good practice and the artist receives more offers of work and the day is repeated several times in other schools.

In the June 2003 issue of a magazine produced by the United Kingdom organisation NESTA[3] creativity is defined as: 'seeing what no one else has seen, thinking what no one else has thought and doing what no one else has dared'. Imagination is cited as a prerequisite of creativity. Another UK group, the National Advisory Committee on Creative and Cultural Education (NACCCE)[4], defines creativity as 'imaginative activity fashioned to produce outcomes that are both original and of value'. A list of qualities which might be thought of as features of creativity include tolerance of ambiguity, playfulness with ideas, materials and processes, teasing and worrying a problem, unlikely connections and juxtapositions, self awareness, the self confidence to take risks and the confidence to be intuitive[5]. Look back over the three examples of primary school art activities above and make your own judgements about how creative they are in the light of the references in this paragraph.

Of course, the children to a greater or lesser extent experienced art in a positive way in the three examples cited. They all enjoyed themselves, they all practised using materials in one or more ways and in

the first two examples, they were introduced to skills of either drawing or painting. In the third example, they discovered something about contemporary art in Britain and certainly realised that sculpture was about much more than statues on plinths. In the second example, knowledge of tone helps children to see how to draw. Looking for tone whilst drawing a portrait will involve looking at shadows that are cast on the head; this is called modelling which in turn gives the drawings a sense of three dimensions. This experience, if reinforced by the teacher will help children draw other subjects from observation. They are clearly learning skills. Is this not part of being creative? There are other positive outcomes. In the first example, the finished sunset paintings were so vibrant and visually successful that when the children took them home a number of parents called the school to say that they had had them framed and hung in the home, much to the pride and delight of the child.

This book does not set out to cover the kind of ground described in our three examples. It will not provide a step-by-step, tip-by-tip, formula for creating a picture, for example. There are numerous how to paint and how to draw books to do that. It will not cover strategies for teaching children about the visual elements or cover how to teach basic skills, although there will be plenty of advice about where to find this information.[6] Also, this book will not describe projects with artists or art galleries. These are now so numerous and various that they deserve a series of books on their own.

So how does this book deal with creativity? By describing how teachers can construct spaces or precincts for children's own ideas. These precincts (the project structures) are designed, for example,

to value originality, to allow a playfulness with ideas, to encourage an exploration of how process can be used to communicate expressive meaning, to promote unlikely juxtapositions and connections, to allow risk taking, to give control over content to children, and to open a space for intuition. However, these values will only be practical if the boundaries, rules and parameters set by the teacher offer enough support to the child. So there are rules and boundaries but these define a supportive skeletal structure within which or upon which, children create their own ideas and over which they have control. The teacher (or the artist, art education specialist, gallery educator, advisory teacher etc.) does not impose the content, the meaning, of what the child creates. The vehicle that carries the possibilities of these meanings is the imaginary cultures and mini societies that children create as a result of taking part in the project.

It is hoped that the projects and mini projects are described in enough detail and with enough clarity to enable any teacher, regardless of her experience, to try them out, and that by showing rather than telling, that teachers will come to see and then to intuit what may work well in their own class. The precincts, the mental spaces for creativity and cultural awareness that the teacher sets out for her children, should be secure environments within which children can learn, understand, create, express and play.

Dream collage, page 104

How the book
is structured

This is a book about practices and is not a book about theories. There is no overt intention to describe a particular curriculum model. These practices are bound by rules and restrictions and governed by parameters, some of which are barely negotiable; for example, the teacher may be working in a particular school with a class of a certain size. There may be budget restrictions on the materials that can be used. There will be other, more pressing priorities.

However, in terms of content, the teacher is responsible for the limits and boundaries of the work. These boundaries are negotiable (creative children may push against limits) but are under the control of the teacher. It is helpful to think of the space they define as a precinct. If the teacher has introduced a project with a broad theme of beliefs then it is unlikely she will accept a child working on ideas inspired by mechanical cogs and gears on a bicycle. In other words, a child's interest in the mechanics of the cogs and gears lies outside the expected boundaries of the project. Which, confusingly, is not to say that a creative child may have stepped outside the project structure and seen an imaginative link between the bicycle and beliefs.

Notwithstanding the last example, this book could be thought of as being about the nature of the boundaries the teacher sets as she plans a project. It is this that defines the teaching and what is taught. For example, consider a maths lesson. It is as if the boundaries for the practice of the child, which clearly restrict him to the problems he is working on, are very tightly defined in two dimensions. The child must work through the examples and apply specifically what he has just been taught to their solution. There is no room for manoeuvre. Arts projects should be different. The boundaries and rules that define the child's practice need to be clear

enough for the child to feel confident about what is being asked of him and supported in his work. However, the space that they describe might be considered multi-dimensional in that there may be almost limitless room for the child to manoeuvre within the precinct of ideas the teacher has defined. It is this definition, the thoughtful setting of boundaries that define a space in which the children's ideas can flourish, that is reliant on the professional skill of the teacher. The fact that the child has a multi-dimensional space in which to create and express ideas does not mean that the teacher is not in control. It is the way that the teacher is in control (and what the teacher is and is not in control of) that is the issue.

The best way to discover what all this might mean is to read the first fourteen pages of Part 1, 'Creating cultures', up to and including, 'Introducing children to patterns from other cultures'. Next, read the introduction. Then read the next few pages about the book's structure and the existing curriculum. Finally, dip into more of the book.

Much of the book consists of a series of detailed descriptions of classroom projects. Following the Introduction and this section, 'Ideas about how to use this book', the reader will find that the classroom projects have been divided into three sections: Part 1, 'Creating cultures'; Part 2, 'Identity, imagination and dreams' and Part 3, 'Beliefs, politics and living with

Dream paintings, page 100

other people'. Each part provides examples of how projects or even individual lessons can be sequenced to create larger projects. However, each of the smaller projects is complete in its own terms and with a little preparation, teachers would be able to pick individual ideas from the book and adapt them for use in their own schemes of work. On the other hand, the overarching intention is to promote the idea that the outcomes of art and design are better when meaningful and that primary school children can create and control these meanings if they are supported in appropriate ways by their teacher. This support involves creating a structure for projects that allows children incrementally to develop related ideas. These become increasingly significant as they create, for example, imaginary cultures, imaginary personalities or even imaginary beliefs. All the usual art skills and processes are relevant and many are referenced. The nature of this way of working is inevitably cross-curricular and the text often includes examples of other arts related activities including writing, dance, music and performance.

Part 1, 'Creating cultures' includes ideas about how to help children work together in groups to invent imaginary cultures in imaginary societies. As children develop these communities, they express their imaginary lives in different ways and create shared meanings, which enable a powerful identification with their work. Each community can produce cultural outcomes such as art and design, creative writing, the spoken word, the media, as well as opportunities for music, dance, drama, festivals and carnival. Children can go on to discover art from other cultures, both imaginary and real.

Part 2, 'Identity, imagination and dreams', focuses on the individual. Classroom projects and activities are inspired by the inner world. Meaning is found as children are asked to work with ideas about what makes up a person's character and how emotions, feelings and thoughts are expressed. Engaging with ideas about dreams opens up possibilities for the imagination to create almost endless variations on the real world. Ideas about imagination and personality are extended to both the animate and inanimate including animals and machines. As a few individuals (friends) come together, they often form much smaller cultural units with particular norms, rules, behaviours and meanings of their own. As in Part 1, outcomes include visual art and design, creative writing and the spoken word, the media, as well as opportunities for music, dance, and drama.

The final part of the book, Part 3, is called 'Beliefs, politics and living with other people'. The two concepts that inspire Parts 1 and 2, communities and the individual, are bought together. Meaning is found through attempts to live together and make sense of who and what we are. For example, children are invited to create imaginary tenets of belief. All religions, including the more ancient animist beliefs, have inspired art. This is an ideal opportunity to help children understand more about different religions and their beliefs. As societies evolve, political issues, the environment and the communities in which we live form the basis for ideas that are endlessly argued about. Art offers children unexpected perspectives as they are asked to form and express ideas through media other than words. The classroom projects are illustrative of structures that could be created by the teacher to give purpose and meaning to the children's art inspired by these fundamental concerns. To turn this the other way around, the children's art outcomes are expressions and catalysts for a range of ideas and ways of thinking that mirror who we are and the way we live. A technique centred on 'key ideas' (see page 135) could be used to support planning these kinds of projects.

Linking ideas

The ideas featured in Part 3 often naturally flow out of those from Part 1 or Part 2. Ideas in Part 2 could be built into projects in Part 1 or Part 3. Specific projects in Part 1 could become part of Parts 2 and 3. All in all, the book does not necessarily need to be read sequentially, and the projects do not necessarily have to be taught in the order they are presented. For example, if children have created imaginary island communities and begun the process of expressing ideas about these communities in cultural ways, they will be enthusiastic about going on to discuss the beliefs they hold, the way they worship or the ways they might celebrate a religious event. Children who have developed the cultural expressions of imaginary urban boroughs will want to go on to think about how to plan a play area for young children or design a piece of street sculpture for everyone to enjoy.

Illustrations

The book is illustrated by examples of work made by primary school children from Year 1 to Year 6 (5 to 11 years-old). In parts 1–3 all of the children's art is shown in close association with text describing the particular project and is not captioned. All images in the introduction and appendix or from other sources are directly acknowledged by captions.

Existing concepts in primary school art curriculum

Skills and processes

Children need skills and an understanding of processes to make quality outcomes and to better express ideas. The author and publisher have taken the view that to include detailed advice here about how to teach art skills such as painting, printing, sculptural construction or drawing would make the book over long and unwieldy. Moreover, good guidance already exists in other publications and on the Internet. To help teachers find this advice, references are made to the units of work on the web site of the United Kingdom's premier organisation for art education, the National Society for Education in Art and Design, at www.nsead.org. At the time of writing in 2005, teachers and schools can have free access to these units by subscribing to START, the magazine for primary and pre-school teachers of art, craft and design. For more information about how to subscribe and current subscription rates call the NSEAD on +44 (0)1249 714825 or visit www.nsead.org.

The visual elements

Concepts such as Line, Tone, Shape, Colour, Texture, Pattern, Space and Form have been used by teachers to help children make art. For example, looking for light and focusing on shadows will help children make tonal drawings. Learning about how colours mix and about primary, secondary and tertiary colours are ways of helping children use a richer variety of colour when they paint. This author's first publication, 'Teaching Art at Key Stage 1' (1993), contains some basic ideas about how to teach the visual elements to young children. The visual elements are also used as starting points for projects in 'Teaching Art at Key Stage 2' (1995). Just as with advice about core skills and processes, detailed ideas about teaching art through the visual elements are not included as part of this book. There are other publications where teachers can find this advice and again, readers are invited to use the units of work compiled by the author at www.nsead.org.

Understanding art

The projects in this book are designed to help children understand more about how people come together to create and express culture. Inevitably, children create meaning that inspires a range of artistic expression and that characterises their imaginary cultures. If teachers go on to introduce these children to examples of actual art, craft and design, children will more readily grasp why the art looks the way it does, in other words, what it means. Ideas about working with art from different cultural backgrounds are woven into the projects. However, in most cases, examples are introduced after the children have been working for a while, rather than at the start. This is part of a more general intention not to influence the art children create with external adult stimuli before they have worked through a process of creating their own ideas. However, there is a chicken and egg syndrome here. It could be argued that the more often a culture is open to and absorbs a range of other cultural expressions, the greater the potential richness of its own cultural products. There is no fixed formula about what to introduce and when.

More themes in the primary school art curriculum

How do the more traditional themes in primary school art fit in? For example: observed landscape is a feature of understanding and recording the environment; portraits are clearly linked to ideas about the individual; architecture can be created by children for imaginary communities or as places of worship, which are part of the expression of imaginary beliefs; the built environment could be an indication of wealth or poverty and become a focus for work centred on political issues. Teaching children about colour and pattern and the other visual elements could easily become part of projects about imaginary communities.

Skills based curriculum models may suggest teachers should be teaching printing in one term, painting in another and three-dimensional work after that. Using the advice in this book does not involve throwing the baby out with the bath water. Paintings, prints and work in clay will be stronger and mean more to the children if they take part in creating imaginary cultural identities.

Children can still record from experience and imagination; they are clearly involved in questioning starting points and selecting ideas. Many of the projects involve collecting visual and other information. Within the projects in Parts 1, 2 and 3, children will be using a variety of approaches to communicate observations, ideas and feelings. Much of what they will go on to do involves designing images and artefacts. Children will be comparing ideas, methods and approaches in each others' work, particularly as they discover how other imaginary communities will have created very different ideas, even within the same classroom. There will always be opportunities to develop more ideas into further work as cultures, even imaginary ones, tend to have a life of their own. Children will understand and so come to know much more about the roles and purposes of artists, craftspeople and designers working in different times and cultures. Children will work on their own; they will collaborate with others on projects in two and three dimensions and in different scales. Starting points will include themselves, their experiences, images, stories, drama, music and the natural and made environment. Projects include a wide range of materials and process, as well as ICT. Visits to art galleries and museums, working with artists, exploring books and the Internet will also enrich many of the activities.[1]

Enjoyment
At the very least, it is hoped that this book is enjoyable to dip into and that it will spark a few ideas. Above all teaching the arts should be great fun.

Notes
1 Readers may recognise references to the National Curriculum for Art and Design, England, in its current form at the time of writing in 2005.

Imaginary animals
page 112

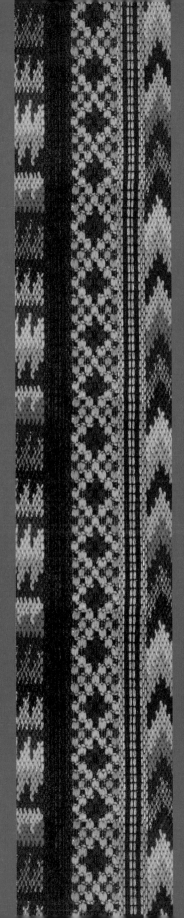

1 Creating cultures

How can we help children create an imaginary culture in the classroom? How can this process of creating a cultural identity give a boost to children's creativity and enable a deeper understanding of other real cultures and societies? Part 1 uses an imaginary island as a centre point around which a whole host of mini projects can be planned. In the book, these small projects are connected together in a kind of narrative. This will suggest that teachers could take children on a creative journey that includes quite a few activities and art processes. The work is inevitably cross curricular. The intention is to show an example of what is possible. It is not to suggest that the mix and match of projects is fixed or that the specific detail of some of the teaching strategies is inevitable.

Although the island theme is dominant through this first part of the book, as you read consider other themes which have the potential to create imaginary cultural meaning. Part 1 briefly considers imaginary worlds and imaginary cities. You could add to this list animal communities, toy worlds, imaginary schools in a neighbourhood, sports clubs, villages, an imaginary nation, gangs (not necessarily with a negative connotation), groups who speak different languages. Part 3 looks at shared imaginary beliefs, political parties and real community issues. Part 2 suggests ideas about individual identity which is inextricably entwined in the identities of the cultures and communities to which we belong. So, projects from the second and third parts of this book could be integrated into Part 1.

In contrast to an extended project, you may only wish to teach a relatively short sequence of activities that marry with your own teaching style and specific curriculum obligations. At the very least 'Creating cultures' should spark some ideas!

Are you going to ask children to create their own imaginary island or is it better if the teacher sets the scene by designing an island to talk about with the children? This section explores both approaches. The island is going to include different communities – cities, towns, villages and settlements. Children will be able to identify with a particular community on the island. Each will have unique characteristics compared with those created by other groups in the class. Some of these characteristics are physical – geography and climate for example. Others are human and created by the children as they work incrementally towards creating an imaginary mini culture. The project begins here with ideas that could link to geography and in particular, maps. This is useful if it is the children themselves who are going to create the island. If teachers decide to use a pre-planned imaginary island to start the project or if they wish to create a new one to suit their particular children, then look ahead to page 31.

1.1
Creating an imaginary island

Starting by talking about islands

Collect, scan or photocopy some images that show the varying shapes of islands. You may be able to download maps of islands from the Internet, or use maps and atlases. For example, there are many islands around Britain (the Isle of Wight, the Isle of Man, Lundy Island, Anglesey, the Isle of Skye and the Hebrides to name just a few). Britain itself is an island. There are tropical islands, Pacific islands, Arctic and Antarctic islands and islands of every shape size and character in between. The nature of islands (for example, climate, size, terrain) helps to determine the kinds of lives that their inhabitants lead.

Show some of the islands to the children and talk about what makes an island an island. Make a list of the advantages and disadvantages of living on an island.

What would it be like living on a small island?
What would it be like living on a tropical island?
What would it be like living on a deserted island?
What kinds of problems might you have if you live on an island?

Talk about the coastal features of islands. For example, can the children find bays, beaches, a peninsula, rocky coastlines, cliffs, river mouths? The children will now be ready to create an island shape of their own.

The whole project could take a different turn in the rest of this section if you asked each group of children to imagine they had been shipwrecked on an island. For example, how would they survive on day one? Each group in the class could go on to create an imaginary community that explores the island (they could make a map that develops as they explore). They could find a place to live and learn how to organise their daily lives. All kinds of problems and issues could be encountered. Many of the ideas in Part 1 of this book, 'Creating cultures', and in Part 3, 'Philosophy, religion and the politics of living with others', could spin off from here.

Drawing a map of an imaginary island together

Perhaps a number of different children can take it in turns to draw different parts of the coastline (the outline) of an island. Remind them about how coastlines appear on maps and about the coastal features such as beaches and river mouths, which they may have already discovered. Why not create a large island that could form the focus of a display by using A1 size paper or card?

When the coastline is finished, add in some of the inland geographical features. You could brainstorm all the different possibilities: a river, high mountains, a lake, a volcano, hills, a plain, a swamp, jungle, grasslands, a waterfall, desert, etcetera. Look at some maps of real islands for ideas.

You could consider asking children to invent the kinds of symbols for the features that they could draw on to the map. This activity might include researching and collecting examples of the graphic conventions used by different kinds of maps. Try to include the kinds of illustrative maps often used in tourism. Children may be able to borrow examples of illustrative tourist maps that have been bought back home after weekend visits and holidays.

Before the children work on completing the map, divide them into groups. Each group will become a

community, settlement, village, town or tribe that lives somewhere on the island. You could allocate a section of the island to each group. They will have to decide where their settlement is going to be. Near a volcano, by a lake, on the beach, near a river, on the coast, in the desert? You may need to influence some of the decisions. It would not be such an interesting island if all the settlements were on the beach or under a volcano. Once there is some variety in ideas about where the different communities are going to be located, the children, one group at a time, can fill their part of the map with their chosen geographical features.

What is the name of your tribe, village, town or settlement?
What is the name of your island?

These illustrated maps can become significant products in themselves. There are many other ideas that could be added. Children could mind map the possibilities. For example, if there is a jungle, what does the jungle contain? Animals? Birds? Butterflies? Different trees and plants? Spirits? If there is a volcano, what additional details could be illustrated? Fire? Lava flows? Geysers? Hot springs? Craters? If there is a river, are there fish? Herons? Fishing boats? Bridges? The children could use oil pastels or felt pens and the island could end up completely

covered in colour. Ask them to add in a representation of the sea around the island to complete the graphic design. Teachers and children who are comfortable with a computer graphics package could draw their map and design symbols, labels and a key, entirely on the computer.

As an alternative approach, draw the outline of the imaginary island yourself onto a large sheet of paper or card. Cut the paper (and therefore divide the island) into five or six segments depending on the number of groups in the class. Give each of the groups some basic guidelines (for example, your area includes a volcano) and ask them to fill in all the characteristics of their part of the island. The children can then bring the sections together and reassemble them to reform the whole island. Talk about the various different ways children have thought about their areas and how they used symbols and images to draw the map. Once the map is reassembled, what kinds of features could be added that would link the different parts together?

Whatever technique is used to create the imaginary island map, the children will now need to brainstorm or mind map simple characteristics of an imaginary settlement, town or village that will become the home for their group. Look at the next three pages for ideas.

Starting with a map drawn by the teacher

If a teacher wished for tighter control over the nature of the island and the settlements, she might draw her own map and create some short profiles for each of the communities. The illustration above is of an imaginary island designed as part of teacher in-service training programme. Ten communities are illustrated since there were to be ten groups working on the project. You might use this map, or you might draw a similar one yourself, limiting the number of communities to the number of groups in the class. As examples, here are the ten profiles that were created for this map. If you are going to use these as starting points for your own island project you may need to adapt them to suit the age of the children you teach.

Kabú is a remote settlement in the rain forest. Huge trees surround the village and it is very wet and very hot. The inhabitants know many secrets of the forest. These include the best plants for healing, how to cure snakebites and how to imitate the sounds of birds.

Karakatán lies on the south side of *El Mombolo*, a great and powerful volcano. The town is very old and the people have ancient skills including how to smelt and forge metal using the heat from the lava. The volcano erupts regularly. Although life is not easy in *Karakatán* the people who live there are respected for their strength and bravery.

Rocasblancas nestles amid the white mountains near the centre of the island. The people are skilled at mining for silver and gold. Although *El Mombolo* dominates the beautiful views from the town, the eruptions have always thrown rocks and ash away from *Rocasblancas*. The inhabitants are wealthy and are expert at buying and selling precious metals. They also trade in other goods at their colourful market.

Incanta lies in gently rolling hills and is surrounded by cherry trees. Almost every family owns a cherry orchard and apart from cherries, they grow apricots and peaches. In spring the mass of white and pink cherry blossom is a wonder to behold and people often talk about the fragrant 'snow' of *Incanta* as gentle winds blow the blossom from the trees. The people of *Incanta* have lovely singing voices.

Porto Bravo is the largest town on *Illuzia*. It is a port and there are people from every other community on the island who live and work there. There are also workers from *Balla Balla* on the mainland 200km away. There are docks and cranes to unload ships, offices, shops and lots of traffic. The inhabitants of *Porto Bravo* are very good at sport especially football. However, there is also more crime in *Porto Bravo* than all the other communities put together.

Ortango is a village in the desert. As you can imagine it is very hot and dry. Getting enough water has always been a problem and the inhabitants are renowned for their ability to find water, dig wells and build pipes out of clay. There are cacti and rattlesnakes. Some families know the secret of how to combine snake venom with juice from cacti to make a powerful magic potion, which they claim allows you enter the spirit world.

Rrahaha is by a lake fed by the largest river on the island. There are abundant fish and river shrimps. The people also keep sheep and cows on the low hills behind the village. In the rainy season there are often floods. The people of *Rrahaha* are the best cooks and eat the best food of anyone on the island. In short, they adore all aspects of food!

Malexa lies amidst fertile grasslands not far from the mouth of the river. Traditionally, the people of the town had wheat farms and were renowned bakers of fine breads. However, in recent times, the charismatic young mayor has attracted investment from high tech industries from overseas and there are now factories making mobile phones and lasers. There are sometimes arguments between the young reformers and older traditionalists.

Pezango is set at one end of a long beach of golden sand. There are palm trees and tropical birds. The village is still a little isolated but is attracting surfers who come for the excellent waves and relaxed and friendly atmosphere. The villagers are good fisherman and know how to find and catch octopus.

Lumulu is found at the extreme south east of the island. There are high cliffs, rocky coves and the famous *Los Gigantes* offshore. There are many different sea birds and their cries resonate and echo the whole day long. The people of *Lumulu* have a huge respect for the sea; they can navigate by the stars and operate a lifeboat, which has rescued many sailors from the base of the treacherous *Los Gigantes*.

You could also decide to create a set of characteristics for the whole island. For example, there might be earthquakes, torrential rainstorms and tidal waves. Some of the history of the island might be relevant. For example, there could have been wars in times past that have left disputes between different parts of the island. Villagers on a remote corner actually arrived as refugees by boat and speak a different language. Archaeologists have discovered the remains of an ancient and long forgotten civilisation. There are fossilised remains of an enormous lizard creature in a far corner of the rain forest. All the communities could share knowledge of these kinds of imaginary 'facts'.

After dividing children into groups (five or six in each seems to be a good number) talk with the whole class about the island and the project. Explain that each group is going to become a community that lives in one of the settlements, towns or villages on the island. Discuss the island in general. Give each group the outline information about their community. You may feel that you do not want to give children too much information about other communities at this stage, as part of the activity might be the way children find out about these other imaginary places during the project.

Imaginary worlds, imaginary cities

Apart from islands, what other themes could be used to inspire a similar scenario? An imaginary world (for example, a planet) could include five or more continents. Each continent has its own unique set of characteristics that are suggested by the teacher in much the same way as the island communities.

Here is an example of how the same project could start with ideas about an imaginary world, with some descriptions of the continents that could be created by children, the teacher or a combination of both. This project could include references to science fiction in both literature and film.

Imagine a world that orbits three suns. There are no oceans of water but instead great seas of green gas divide the continents. Unlike our world space travellers regularly visit some of the inhabitants.

Algae cover the continent of *Verdia*, which glows all possible shades of very bright greens. The algae covers the whole surface in a thick, soft layer, The intelligent beings who live there have developed modern cities which float on the algae supported by huge rafts of a sponge like substance that is made from combining the excrement of an enormous white and black bird with a special yellow liquid found below the algae layer.

Electrica straddles the equator and is composed of sharp mountains of a diamond like mineral and lakes of the green gas. The inhabitants live under the lakes in vast caverns that sparkle with light from minerals. There are three huge underground cities; these depend on a different kind of energy from other continents. They store energy from lightning strikes on the mountain peaks in naturally occurring rocks that act like batteries.

The majority of *Vacas* is a continent of very fertile flat, light blue grasslands. Many small clouds of the green gas form and disperse leaving tiny amounts of a turquoise residue that contains a rich supply of nutritious food. Huge herds of cow-like creatures use multi-mouthed heads to suck up the residue from the tips of the blades of grass. Many of the towns and cities on *Vacas* built their wealth on farming these herds and then selling food products.

Portoia is a small but rich continent that is positioned at one of the poles. The climate is cooler than the rest of the planet and the green gas sometimes crystallises into a brittle but iridescent series of iceberg like lumps. The people have a long history of welcoming space travellers and they have built an elaborate spaceport that is connected to the surface by fast transit lifts. *Portoias* are very different from inhabitants on the other continents. They speak many space languages and often travel to other planets.

The continent of *Eclectia* is the most mixed of all the great landmasses on the imaginary world and it occupies the largest area. It could be said to include a little of the characteristics of all the other continents. There are many different cities, towns and villages. What ties the people together is their love of colour. All over *Eclectia* colours are displayed in every possible form.

Even though this imaginary world is quite different from our imaginary island, you could follow an almost identical structure to the project. Just adapt the sessions that follow to the ideas that children have created. Look back at ideas about creating maps: you could use very similar ways of working to create a map or maps of the world and its continents.

An imaginary city could include five or more suburbs, boroughs or districts. The city itself will have general characteristics. It could be a port, on a great river, surrounded by mountains, near volcanoes, etcetera. Each group of children is to imagine they live in one of the boroughs. What are the characteristics of each part of the city? How is life in one borough different compared to the next?

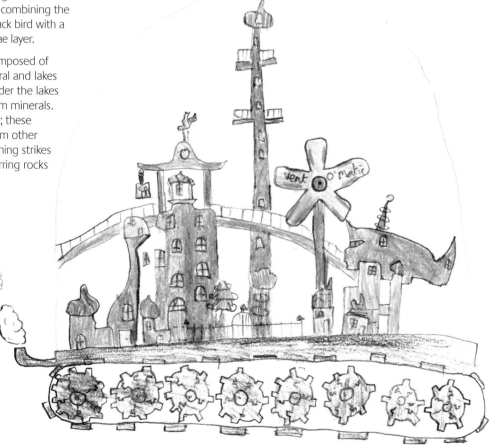

1.2
Patterns and motifs

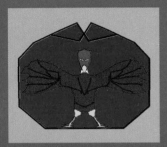    

The island and its communities form the basis of all the work that follows. The teacher has provided an open ended but secure environment for imaginary ideas, a kind of precinct, within which children will feel confident to be playful and creative. They will feel a sense of ownership. It is helpful to think of the island as a three-dimensional or even multi- dimensional ideas space. This means that there is almost no end to the depth or possible layering of any new ideas that follow. Mind-mapping the project is quite an efficient way of developing its potential. For example, thinking about the village of Lumulu (see page 32), almost every family has a boat. This idea could be expanded. What problems are there if you own a boat? What are the solutions? What are some of the stories from the past about strange events that have happened in and around boats? What are the boats for? Boats, sails, flags, nets, anchors and ropes are used as designs on tableware and on fabrics. What do these look like?

In the summer, there is a festival of boats. What happens? Is there a special song about boats, or a dance or activity that is performed at the festival? Do local artists make paintings and drawings of the boats? Each of these idea spaces could be starting points for more creative thinking and activity. Of course, the inhabitants of Lumulu could also be great experts on the wandering albatross. How would a branch of a mind-map look with large and mysterious wandering sea birds as its inspiration! Looking back over this paragraph you could chart all the possible projects for the classroom. In effect, the children and teacher will be creating a mini culture or faux culture where different forms of expression are used to communicate with others. Look back to page 14 and the introduction for more ideas about culture. »146

Brainstorming or mind-mapping ideas about your settlement

Designing a motif

The children will work in groups to answer the kinds of questions that follow. These questions could also form the main branches of a mind-map.

What do you do for work?
What do you do in your spare time? How do you relax?
What do people wear?
Where does your food come from? What do you eat?
At your annual festival, what do you celebrate? Why?
How do you celebrate?
What is difficult about life in your community?
Are there any special problems that your community has to overcome?
What are the best things about life in your community?

Each of the areas above could be further developed. For example, consider the possibilities of clothing.

What do you wear for work?
What do you wear in your spare time?
Is there special clothing for festivals and celebrations?
Do important people or leaders wear anything special?

To help children to focus on even more detail we could take one example and expand this again. For example, what is worn for a festival?

What do you wear on your head?
What do you wear on your feet?
How would you describe what you wear on your body?
What are the clothes made of?
What are the colours, patterns and designs like?
Do you wear any jewellery or body adornments? What are they like?
Do wear any belts or other accessories? What are they like?

A motif, symbol or logo could become a visual mark of the community. There are many examples of this that you could show children. Countries often have national symbols – the Welsh dragon or Scottish thistle, for example. Companies invent visual logos to help identify their character. The Michelin man and the Little Chef symbol are examples – there are many others. Throughout history, symbols have been a part of heraldry and have been included on flags and pennants. Each settlement, village or town on the island could have its own motif and during the designing process, children may create other visual ideas that they will find useful as the project develops.

Ask the children to work in their groups. Ask them to briefly re-visit their ideas about their imaginary communities. What kinds of motifs could they create that might symbolise these? For example, if they lived in Lumulu they might list everything they could think of to do with boats, seabirds, and anything else that came up. Ask them to brainstorm ideas in two different ways. First, using words they could list under various ideas. Second, they could do a visual brainstorm, drawing ideas rather than writing. They could combine the two methods.

Ask the children to make a shortlist of the best ideas. Ask them to think of the meaning behind each idea. For example, have they chosen an idea because it is used as part of a celebration or is it a feature of every day life in their community? Let's imagine that the people of Karakatán created ideas about eagles. Eagles are often seen flying above the town and they are strong brave birds important to the people.

Suppose they have chosen a flying eagle as a possible motif, could they find some images of eagles in flight in books or on the Internet? These can be drawn, photocopied, digitally photographed, scanned and printed. They might make quite a large collection of flying eagles. Ask them to make some very simplified drawings of their favourite eagle. Remind them again that motifs are often simplified. They often have a few clear bold outlines, shapes, lines and colours.

Children might draw using felt pens. One method could be to use very thin white photocopy paper. The children could trace the basic shape of the flying eagle that they can see through the photocopy paper using a pencil and then re-draw and simplify the image again with bold felt pen lines, rubbing out the pencil marks when they have finished. Alternatively, if children already possess some skills, they could scan, trace and transform a digital image of a flying eagle using the computer and appropriate software.

Perhaps children could work on their own best motif idea to produce a finished design. The group could then vote on the one that will be used for their community. However, all the ideas could be very useful in later work. **»146**

Creating patterns

As soon as children start talking about the kinds of ideas generated by the imaginary island they will have begun to create an imaginary culture. Immediately opportunities for artwork abound. This project focuses on creating patterns, which can be applied in many different ways. Look ahead to page 54 and the section about designing for the home to see where this project could lead.

Revise the idea of pattern with the children. One method might be to collect examples of different patterns to show the children. Repetition is the most important feature of pattern. These repetitions can take many forms. Colours, shapes, motifs and lines can be repeated regularly or irregularly. It is helpful if the children see diverse patterns so that you can explain just how wide the choice is, but not necessarily an arbitrary selection. As always, finding a simple structure will help the children make their own creative decisions later. For example, you could show children patterns from different categories such as animals, plants, food, science, fabrics, buildings and mathematics. On the other hand, you might divide the categories into patterns with repeating colours and shapes or irregular and regular repetitions. The characteristics of the community itself might suggest the kinds of patterns children should look at or research.

If you think the children need to practise the ideas that surround the general concept of pattern, why not devise a simple preliminary exercise? Here are a few ideas:

- Use a camera to record patterns inside and outside the classroom.
- Use a sketchbook to collect patterns inside and outside the classroom.

- Research in the library, find examples of regular and irregular patterns, and record these by photocopying, scanning or drawing.
- Make some small drawings of natural and patterns designed by people.
- Find the simplest pattern you can and a then find the most complicated pattern.
- Make a display of the many different kinds of pattern you have collected.

Why not show children how to make and use templates? Choose one of the motifs from the previous project that has a simple shape and glue a drawing, printout or photograph on to a piece of thin card. Cut out the shape to make the template. This can be used to draw around and in this way, children can repeat the same basic shape many times. Using this method the image also can be overlapped, rotated or reflected very easily. Children could also use a digital image and computer graphics software to do the same exercise on screen, repeating their image in different ways. A photocopier can be used to create repeats of the same image and the same digital photograph could be printed several times. Software that helps to print digital pictures often offers a mosaic option. However they are generated, these paper images could be cut out and collaged to create a pattern.

The first and easiest pattern for the children to make will be one based on their motif. For example, using the idea of the flying eagle on page 34, how could the shape of the motif (in this case the eagle) be repeated to make a pattern? Colours could be repeated, as could other decorative ideas, such as smaller shapes and lines (feathers for example), forming more detail inside or around the eagle shape. They could create their experimental pattern

ideas freehand and in rough, perhaps exploring several different possibilities before selecting one to draw more carefully.

Patterns can be abstract too. Shapes, lines, textures can all be repeated to create pattern. Patterns inspired by mathematics could also be introduced. Ask the children to think of two, three or four colours that they think would be the most appropriate for their community. For example, children might choose three different greens, which represent the natural world for the imaginary people who live in the rain forest. The three greens will be repeated in the pattern. Other children may choose darker colours as they live underground, with black being the most significant colour of all!

To inspire children you could show them some examples of patterns from all the different categories and types of pattern that were collected at the start of this project. Remind them to think about their communities. They will generate more ideas and more ideas that are original, if they talk about the possibilities first. Be prepared to field questions, support ideas and sooth doubts without suggesting too strongly, what the children should do. Perhaps combining pictorial elements with abstract ones will make the most interesting patterns. Children will happily combine shapes, lines and colours with repeated recognisable images.

If they have not already done so, children should go on to add their chosen colours to the pattern. Remind them again about repeating colours. Although, they could have a regular repeating pattern with random colours! »146

Using pattern in art and design

After they have created a number of pattern ideas or after the patterns are finished, ask the children how they could use the patterns in their communities. Where could the patterns be seen? On tableware, fabrics, clothing, walls, banners, carpets? This may prompt you to develop the project into a skills-based activity such as printing, using textiles or working in clay. For example, look forward to page 54 and the section on designing for the home. Here are some ideas, some of which are developed later in the book although you may decide not to have a very finished looking end product at this stage.

- Make a frieze out of long strips of thin non-glossy card (some children will find it useful to start with coloured card) and ask the children to make a good version of their pattern along the strip. If they are using white card, it may well look better if they can add colour to the 'background'.

The frieze could be used to border a display all about the community. The strips can also be combined, one above another, to create a block of different patterns.

- Fold an A4 sheet of thin card to A5 and ask the children to draw a version of their pattern on the front. This is going to be a greetings card. They could write text for the inside that is relevant to their imaginary people, beliefs and religion. They might invent a special celebration where sending cards to family and friends is part of the tradition. Look forward to page 118 and ideas about creating imaginary beliefs, which could go on to inspire a greetings card design.
- Create a piece of fabric using the pattern. The simplest way is to use fabric crayons or fabric paint. Another technique would be to scan a finished pattern design and print this onto special

transfer paper that could be ironed onto material. A project using cold water paste resist is described later in this chapter.

- Make some tiles in clay and ask the children to decorate their tile with their pattern to create a ceramic frieze or panel with their pattern.

However far you decide to take the pattern project, it might now be worthwhile pausing to allow the different groups in the class to talk about their communities and show some of the other children their patterns. Where have the ideas behind the patterns come from? How is each community going to use their pattern design? What do children think about the patterns from other communities? After looking at the patterns can they say which have the best qualities from their point of view. In other words, what makes a successful pattern?

Introducing children to patterns from other cultures

When is it a good time to show children examples of art, craft and design associated with the work they are doing? There are three rather obvious choices: at the start of the project, in the middle of the project, at the close of the project. Indeed, whole projects may have art from other cultures at their centre. Teachers and children take inspiration from looking at, talking about and investigating art works. The meaning of the children's work is centred on the work of other artists. In this book, we are placing emphasis on helping children create ideas of their own that are to a lesser (rather than a greater) extent dependent on ideas introduced by adults. Therefore, in this case we are going to introduce children to patterns from other different cultures after they have created their pattern ideas.

As children create their imaginary communities, they are creating their own imaginary cultures. This fact facilitates a deeper understanding of the cultural products of different peoples. In the case of our pattern project, children empathise with the people who have created and used patterns, which have come into being as a result of unique ways of life and cultural expressions. Patterns are part of the visual expression of almost every culture. So there are many examples. Options include Maori, Britain in the 1940s, Native American, Islamic, African, Victorian, Andalusian and Egyptian. Personal preference, availability of resources and links with the curriculum will all influence the choice. To illustrate the possibilities, here is an example of how a teacher could introduce children to patterns made by handloom weavers in the Mayan communities of Guatemala.

Woven textiles are emblematic of the art from Guatemala. The vibrant colours and bold designs have evolved through generations of weavers of Mayan descent. In terms of the creating patterns project on page 36, they often combine recognisable motifs with abstract and geometric designs. These abstract motifs sometimes have names that suggest the origin of the pattern. Different villages and different families within different villages, express variations in designs that are unique to them. For example, a bee motif is the centrepiece of one great-grandmother's designs. She had childhood memories of living near a meadow full of bees. Her mother began to incorporate bees into her woven fabrics, she continued the idea, her daughters and granddaughters are now weaving, and embroidering bee motifs in what has become a cultural tradition for this family. The illustration shows a woven fabric that illustrates a number of patterns used by weavers in the small town of San Antonio Aguas Calientes.

The patterns are used to decorate huipils (a traditional smock like garment), skirts, ceremonial shawls, serviettes (which are used to wrap around warm tortillas), ribbons and tzutes (a cloth made from two woven panels and worn folded on the head to support a basket or carry a child). Women and girls who are highly skilled craftspeople use handlooms. Girls begin to learn to weave around the age of seven. By the time they are fourteen, they are often as capable as their mothers. Nowadays, weavers from Aguas Calientes also make weavings to sell to tourists in nearby Antigua, the old capital of Guatemala.

Children could learn a little about Guatemala, its climate and geography and imagine what life might be like for the family who created the weavings illustrated here. If they look for Aguas Calientes on a map, they may discover it is near several volcanoes. The name of the town means 'hot waters'. There are earthquakes. A little research about the way Mayan people live today shows that they are poor by Western European standards.

Having already thought about life in their imaginary communities and having already created a pattern, children are receptive to the kinds of cultural information given by the teacher. They are open to the images of the art works themselves, and more able to see how the unique way the look of the patterns' is linked to the lives of the people who created them.

This example is likely to inspire children to create textile designs of their own for their imaginary communities. Look forward to page 62 at the projects about clothes and fashion, textiles and fabric design. It may also inspire children to learn to weave (see page 56).

1.3 Stories, myths and legends

Creating ideas

If you have followed the imaginary islands theme that runs through Part 1, you will have seen how children can create an imaginary island, draw maps, create communities, design a motif for their specific community, create a pattern and see how that pattern could be used as part of different art and design outcomes. They may have gone on to discover how people have created patterns in different real world cultures.

By now, children will be identifying with their imaginary communities, which will have names and a whole set of invented characteristics, some of which will have been given by the teacher, but most created by the children. There are different ways of both creating and recording the ideas.

Children could be encouraged to take control of a display space near their workstation. As they work, children use masking tape to fix ideas (both visual and textual) to the wall. Images, word lists, mind maps, design ideas and much else can be informally displayed. Children can be encouraged to move elements of this display around, creating new connections and juxtapositions. In the photograph, the teacher has covered the table in lining paper, on which children are able to write and draw, adding more possibilities for spontaneous and unexpected ideas, confirming an atmosphere where idea creation is dominant. Finished products can come later. Another illustration shows a preliminary mind-mapping exercise. The example of a more developed documentary text that follows is from the same class. These show how the teaching strategy has begun to create quite different ideas within the same classroom, as the children create their communities and begin to express their imaginary cultures. Teachers will see the many directions the project could now take. A glance at the contents list will give clues about where to look for more ideas within this publication.

The Jarlo Community
'The Jarlo community live in a huge multi-coloured glass house. It is quite a big settlement it is near a long river. They make beautiful furniture for themselves and some other communities. The Jarlo currency is called Pop Poppers. They sell their furniture for 30 Pop Poppers because it is guaranteed to last 30 years.

Our names are…
Tinky Winky, Dipsy, La La, Poe, Noo-Noo

The weapons that we use are made out of the strongest wood we could find, it is carved by the man and softened by the woman by soaking in the river.

We have a festival called McSing where we celebrate our voices. This takes place on March 12th (the same day as Danny from McFly's birthday!). We celebrate these occasions by having a sea parade in the morning for Danny's birthday, and in the night we have a huge firework display and sing a song that the person you dress up as has sung.

Our God is called Elvis and we sing to him, this is our way of praying. In our spare time we listen to music that is very good to listen to because it helps us sing that song more professional. Some of the music we listen to is McFly, Girls Aloud, Green Day, Destiny's Child and Britney Spears. Another way we relax is by playing instruments.

Jarlo's main eating area is McEaters restaurant it serves food with a twist.

The clothes we wear are quite modern. Each item of clothing has a microphone stiched on in the corner it is showing Elvis that we respect him.

Our biggest problem is that other communities think that we are loud and that music/singing should be banned.'

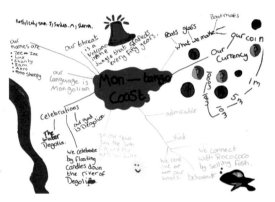

Creating a myth

Different peoples in different parts of the world have their own mythologies, their own legends, folklore and traditional stories. These express many elements of human experience, such as the creation of the world, religious beliefs, the behaviour of animals, and the seasons. Many have a moral message. Some explain the unexplicable, others allay fears. Some myths are more complex and express relationships between the spiritual (the supernatural) and every day existence. Stories humanise religious figureheads such as gods and prophets. All enrich the culture of the people who tell, read, write, enact, sing, dance or dream them. Folklore can also have a central role in the children's imaginary island communities. We can continue to develop the embryonic cultures by creating stories that express something significant for the community. These stories become rich seams of content for new work as visual culture, including print media, film, animation and digital media. Stories also inspire work across the arts – different forms of literature, movement, dance and music. This project describes one way to create a story structure linked to a myth or legend pertinent to the children's imaginary island lives. It is to be set in the imaginary past of their imaginary community.

Start by reminding children about the island and the various communities. These settlements are cities, towns or villages and have a particular geography. The story project involves the creation of characters, a problem to be solved and a journey to embark on to solve the problem. The setting is the island and each community. The teacher could introduce the concepts of magic and fantasy as these may transport the story out of the ordinary.

The children need to invent a problem. For example, is there something that happens linked to natural phenomena like the sea, wind or rain? Have there been, or could there be natural disasters? Is there a person from the past whose actions created a problem for the community? Are there people from outside who come in and create problems? Is there a problem caused by a creature, a god or spirit? Do animals cause problems? The list is endless. In Incanta, for example, (look back at page 32) cherries are being eaten by the greedy larvae of a strange wasp. Perhaps one of the characters causes the problem. Perhaps the problem comes in suddenly from outside the community or has always been there and people have just accepted their fate.

Children could brainstorm or mind-map, first to find the problem and then to describe the many possibilities suggested by the dilemma. If you wish to offer a greater level of support, you could ask them to think, in an organised way, in terms of the kinds of categories of problems suggested in this paragraph or for example:

Why did the problem start?
What causes the problem?
When did the problem start?
Is the problem there the whole time or does it come and go?
What are the worst things about the problem?
What do the people think about the problem?
What can be done about the problem?

In a similar way, children can create characters. One of the characters may already be suggested by the problem. For example, a powerful monkey has stolen the secret of how to make gold from rocks the people mine from the mountain. The monkey could become a character in the story, with strange and unusual powers. It is possible that a mountain, tree, flower or other natural object could be a character – usually these would have a voice and have a part in the action. Clearly a character could be a god or spiritual being of some kind, but characters drawn from the inhabitants of the community might be all that children need.

Although several characters will be necessary, as a rule three main characters are more than enough. Each of the characters can be developed further. For example, the teacher could ask the group to think about appearance, behaviour, abilities, weaknesses, and personality.

To help develop their ideas (with or without the teachers help), they could mind-map or brainstorm each of the characters in turn by considering these questions:

If you met your character what would they be like?
How would you feel?
What would the character look like?
Think about their clothes, their colour, their size and anything else that you could think of.
Would they be carrying anything?

The third key element is the journey that one or more of the characters need to take in order to find a solution to the problem. There will be a start to the journey and an end. What happens on the way? Easy journeys do not tend to make interesting stories. So as well as the central problem that created the momentum for the story, smaller inconveniences emerge on the way. There are many examples of this in literature – think of Bilbo Baggins journey in the Hobbit. Finally, ask the children to create an end to the story, which will include solving the problem. There might be a celebration, a return home or some form of final event.

The children will be full of ideas. They will have been working together, in their communities to create a myth or legend that they share. Ideas may be expressed in rough notes, word lists from brainstorms or as mind maps. You may have asked one child from the group to write out the bare bones of the story in rough. Much will still be in the memory and half formed.

Although a more formal writing exercise could develop from this activity, in the spirit of cultural invention, the next step is to create visual story strips, which are likely to have a mixture of images and words. The strips help children grasp the whole of the story and can lead to a wealth of visual art. They are also excellent tools in helping children with the spoken word and become part of their communities' oral tradition.

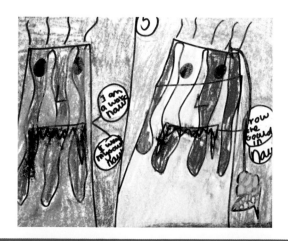

Story strips

Story strips also could be called storyboards. Although at this stage we are not suggesting that they become part of a film or animation project, this is obviously a possibility and is explored later in the book (see page 48).

Cut strips of paper for the children to use. A useful size seems to be A2 folded in half, length ways, and then in half again. The story is going to be rendered with a series of annotated drawings running from left to right.

Each child has a strip. Any graphics media are appropriate. Felt pens, coloured markers and oil pastels give good strong colours. A black roller tipped pen is also useful. You could further divide the strip into six compartments running from left to right. The first box is a kind of introduction and could include the main characters and details of the community, the second shows the problem, the next three show the journey and the final area is for the resolution of the problem. However, you could also let the children decide on the number of separate drawings they think they will need. If they run out of space, they could simply glue or tape an extension to the paper strip. Here is the first way of introducing the activity to children:

Remember your story about a myth or legend? You are going to draw the start of the story on the left hand side of your strip. Your first picture could show the community, the characters and maybe something about the problem? Next, you need to show the journey and what happens along the way. The last box will be the end of the story when the problem is solved.

Don't worry about the drawing. You can use words as well as pictures to help to show what is happening. For example, if you want to include an eagle, but don't feel confident about drawing eagles then draw a kind of eagle shape and use a word or two to tell us what it is supposed to be. You could also write along the bottom of the strip, or along the top. You only have the pens and pastels to draw with. So you can't rub out your mistakes. So be bold and carry on even if things go wrong. Just draw over the mistakes or use words to tell us what is going on.

Draw in outlines first. Try and draw right up to the top of the strip. Add in details later. You could completely fill in the empty spaces with colour.

The second strategy is aimed at a more careful and considered outcome. Give each child two strips; one for ideas and a second for their finished strip. This time give children pencils and erasers.

Remember your story about a myth or legend You are going to draw the start of the story on the left hand side of your strip. So your first picture could show the community, the characters and maybe something about the problem? Then you need to show the journey and what happens along the way. The last box will be the end of the story when the problem is solved.

Use one strip for rough working out and the second for your finished work. You have a pencil and a rubber. Think about each stage of the story as a mini picture. Draw very lightly on your best strip and adjust the picture by rubbing out the pencil lines until you are happy. Then, use felt pens or coloured pencils to go over the lines. Add in detail and

backgrounds. You can use words to add information or tell us about something that is happening that you cannot show by drawing. The words can appear anywhere on the strip. Along the top, the bottom or in the drawing itself.

It is a good idea to test out the ideas on the rough strip. If you need to find an image which will help you with your drawings you can use books or the Internet. For example, you want to draw an eagle, but need an eagle to copy, so look for eagle pictures in the library or the Internet. If need be we can photocopy or print up any pictures you find. You could even collage these images onto your strips. It might be a good idea to do all your research before you start drawing the finished story strip. You can completely colour the strips if you think that they will look better that way.

Use the first strategy to make more rapid progress, especially if you are going to continue with new activities on the story theme. For example, if you are heading towards an animation project or making a video it will be better not to spend too much time on creating very finished end products at this stage.

The work could take another direction and metamorphose into a drawing comics project. In Britain, comics are still sometimes dismissed as a serious art form. This contrasts with France where *les bandes dessinées* and the artists who draw them are hugely respected. Whatever the adult thinks about comics, children will love the work and it is a very useful way to teach them about visual composition. The project could use the first roughly drawn story strips to help children generate ideas for planning a double page for a comic. »146

Creating an oral tradition

This is a rather grand heading for a teaching strategy that uses the story strips to encourage children to speak fluently as they tell others about their community's legend, myth or story. As children practise telling the story it becomes gradually internalised. They will not need any prompts and will speak fluently, with meaning in their voice, and without the need to formally learn a script.

The story strips have all the information the children need. Two children can hold the strip, one on each side, so that the child narrator is looking straight at the drawings and words. Ask the child telling the story to work along the strip from left to right using the pictures and written notes to help her tell the

story. For example, the first box or section may contain the three main characters and have information about the problem. Then the journey begins with everything that happens along the way until a solution is found. The children may be able to inject descriptive snippets as they tell the tale. For example, how a character is dressed, or details about the land they are walking through. Each child can practise in turn.

Children from the same community will tell the story in slightly different ways. This can be a talking point later. Can the children get to a point when they can remember all the details as well as the general structure of the tale without using the story strip as a prompt?

It is great fun to invite children from one community to visit another to tell their stories. After all, they may all live on the same imaginary island! Further work is possible if individual children want to create their own personal stories. Eventually, any myths, legends or stories, whether shared or individual, can be written down.

Television presenting and speaking to video

When children read written text aloud to others they are often hesitant and less than fluent. The need to concentrate on the reading often means that they are not able to communicate what is being expressed as clearly as they might. Speaking clearly and confidently and using expressive modulations in the voice that help carry meaning, is one of the skills needed when talking to a camera. Creating an oral tradition project is a great starting point for a mini project where children learn some simple skills both in front of and behind the camera. Here is an example of how it can work.

Telling stories to a video camera is a useful way to help children focus on the task, record their efforts and teach them some basic skills used by television presenters and reporters, so why not set up an impromptu TV studio? There could be a chair for the child (the story teller) to sit on, a background of some kind and at least one directional light. Set up a video camera on a tripod. Adjust the height. With all but the most expensive cameras, you will need an external microphone that plugs into a port on the camera. This will improve the sound of the child's voice as they tell the story. This mike can be off camera or held by the child telling the story.

The children can work in groups. One child will be the presenter and tell the story; another will be the sound engineer (holding the mike); a third will operate the camera and two further children will operate the cue card (the story strip). There could also be a lighting engineer responsible for the directional light. In this set up, an adult takes on the role of director, but equally this role could also be given to a child.

The children will need to be taught one or two basic skills. The sound engineer or the narrator will need to hold the microphone steady. Any rustling and fidgeting will be picked up on tape. The camera operator will need to check that the microphone is not in the shot (if the mike is off camera) and that the presenter looks good and is well positioned. The teacher could show the children how to use the camera zoom and adjust the height and direction of the camera on the tripod.

The lighting engineer should first turn off the light source. Where are the shadows on the face? For example, if the light is from a window to the right of the child's face, the left hand side will be in shadow. The lighting engineer can position the light to fill in these shadows and improve the look of the face. They will need to make sure that the light source is not so close to the head that it creates new shadows and that the light is off camera. The child story teller (presenter) needs to think about the following:

Do not lean back or slouch in the chair. Sit up leaning slightly towards the camera. This will make you look alert and interested.
Do not let your attention stray, stay looking at the camera and do not let your eyes wander.
Look cheerful, especially when you start and finish. Try starting and ending the story with a smile.
Speak with a normal but strong voice.
Change the inflection and dynamic of your voice. This means making your voice louder and softer and putting emphasis on certain words. Sometimes a word or phrase can be spoken with expression. This will help add atmosphere to the story. Try not to use a flat voice with the same tone all the way through. The listeners could get bored!

The children holding the cue card (the story strip) should hold the strip just above the camera but as close to it as possible without touching. They should start by positioning the first segment of the story just above the camera. As the presenter narrates the story they should gradually move the strip along so that the relevant part is always just above the camera. This way the presenter's eyes will always appear to be looking directly at the camera and so at the viewer.

The story strip is in effect a cueing device. Because children have told the story using pictures and words together and because any text is not presented in a dense blocked way (as on a page of writing) the children will be much more fluent as they tell the tale. They will also be able to remember both the structure of the story and some of the smaller details. They should tell the story in a natural way. However, for the best results they will still need to practise.

You could gradually let everyone in the class take a turn at both being the presenter and taking on some of the other jobs mentioned above. Show the results to the class either on a TV or projected onto a white board or screen. The children will immediately learn how they could improve both their presentation and the story.

There are a number of other projects in this book that focus on broadcast skills. Check out the project on interviews and on compiling a news report (page 131). Television is such a powerful part of our own culture, that helping primary school children understand a little about the kinds of skills needed – and therefore enabling them to be creative with those skills – surely should have a place as part of their arts experiences in school?

Animation

Animation offers children opportunities to experiment with moving images and related sounds. Children can explore the metamorphosis and movement of objects, changing colours and moods, the animation of storyboards and the development of cartoons. Children might discover drawn animation, stop frame animation and computer animation.

Drawn animation is the original form of animation used by makers such as Disney and Warner Brothers. An animator draws and colours each frame of the film by hand, painstakingly changing the expressions and positions of the characters in each drawing. Each individual drawing is then photographed, one image at a time, on to film. When the film is played, the still images run together in our minds to create movement. Flick books are a useful way of explaining how this works.

Stop frame animation involves making three-dimensional characters and moving them and any props bit by bit on a set. Again, the animator records each movement one frame at a time until a film sequence is achieved and all the frames are played together quickly, running forward to make the characters look as if they are moving in real time. Stop frame animators include companies like Aardman Productions in the UK who make the Wallace and Gromit films.

Computer animation is how films like *Finding Nemo* are produced. Computer animation imitates the techniques of drawn animation in that images are created one at a time. However, computer animation allows artists to work very much faster and use all the digital tools available in appropriate software. Often previously tedious tasks can be automated and digitally duplicating images and parts of images

makes the process much less time consuming. In commercial films, improving computer modelling allows animators to create a very high level of detail.

When it comes to the practicality of working in the classroom teachers will need to make compromises. For example, it is possible to show children examples of drawn animation from early Disney cartoons and children could view reproductions of original line drawings (there many available to look at on the Internet). There are also plenty of books with superb illustrations. However, the process of making a drawn animation cartoon takes so long that it is probably more practical to choose another technique. Although, children could easily make a flick book with a simple image like a bouncing ball.

Stop frame animation

If the children are going to make a stop frame animation, they will achieve more if they work together. For example, if we stay with the stories created for the imaginary island then one story could be selected to represent the whole island. Each group of children could work on one scene of the story, which can then be edited together to make a longer and more complete film. Teamwork is a vital part of making any film and children can learn valuable lessons about how they can improve their creative outcomes if they successfully cooperate.

A section on animation is included at this point in this book because children will have already completed the first part of the four stages of an animation project. They have worked on their story and characters and following the exercise in developing an oral tradition will more comfortably write a script for an animated film version.

In terms of stop frame animation, stage two will be the drawing or making of characters and sets or backgrounds for the action. Stage three is the production of the film, either using stop frame or computer animation techniques. The fourth stage is the editing, final additions and addition of a sound track. The illustrations show children using a webcam and inexpensive software to make stop frame animation using Plasticine models and backgrounds of paper and card.

Computer animation

Computer animation software usually has a set of painting tools built in, so that children can draw the individual frames of their animation.

To make animations look smooth children will need to use the same kind of techniques that professional animators use. In particular, when drawing a sequence of frames, an animator would draw the first and last frames on thin translucent paper, then stack them under a new piece of paper on top of a light box (a glass table with a light in), in order to see, through the paper, just how the frame in between should be drawn. Animation software can give the user a 'light box' or 'ghosting' mode, in which the previous and next frames of the film are shown, faded and behind, the one currently being worked on. All the painting tools work as normal when in ghosting mode. They ignore the ghost images but you can still see them and use them as guides. This acts a bit like the layers of translucent paper that the traditional animator uses so he can see how to create a movement or change of expression bit by bit from the same basic drawing. The truth is that teachers who want to use computer animation in the classroom will have to spend some time familiarising themselves with the software. »147

Children can add sound effects to the animation. Some software comes with a collection of noises, and children will also be able to use any sound sample they already have. However, they can even sample new sounds directly into the animation software, if the sampling hardware is available. The process of creating and sampling sounds to add to the animation could become a project all of its own, especially as children may need to fit the sound to the frames. This will involve thinking about timing.

A commentary, or dialogue, involves a similar set of problems to adding sounds. Children will have to time the spoken words to fit the sequence of images. In itself, this is not too difficult a task if the teacher shows them the software tools.

Once you've finished your animation, you can usually save it in formats understood by almost any multimedia package and some software products allow you to print the images as a flick-book, with all the crop-marks ready printed!

1.4
Rhythm, chant, dance and song

Rhythm, chant and simple songs

Although this book has a focus on the visual arts, if the reader accepts the premise that creating mini cultures is one way to empower and inspire children to work meaningfully, then it is important to acknowledge that other art forms, such as music, dance, performance and, as we have already seen, the spoken and written word, are likely to enrich the imaginary cultures children create. In this part of the book ideas about creating communities who live on an imaginary island take centre stage. For example, children may have created patterns and motifs, drawn story strips, designed a comic book spread and worked to tell their story to camera. The characters of the imaginary myths or legends have reinforced the children's sense of the community and they may have already thought about the possibility of special occasions such as celebrations and ceremonies. It is natural to want to include music and dance.

The first project focuses on rhythm. Rhythm is closely allied to pattern. Some teachers teach very young children about visual pattern using rhythms of sounds or movements. The various kinds of rhythmic repetitions can be rendered visually. This sequencing is a valuable conceptual tool for children to learn and practise. »147

For this section, we are going to look at an example of exploring rhythm using words and phrases. These can be developed into chants and songs. The words used will come from the children. There should be a strong association with their imaginary communities.

Ask children to select a number of words that they think are significant to the community. To start with, they could make two lists. One list has words of one syllable, the second words of two syllables. They will need to choose one word from each list that go well together.

For example, children from Rrahaha (see page 32) might choose 'lake' with one syllable and 'river' as a word with two syllables.

Start by saying 'lake' four times slowly, and then repeating the lake, lake, lake, lake pattern a number of times. You could clap to keep a strong beat, perhaps clapping harder on the first of each of the four beats for emphasis. Now keeping to the same beat say the two-syllable word 'river'. Ask the children to place the same weight on each syllable. You will be chanting 'river' four times, pausing and repeating. For every one syllable of 'lake' there are two of 'river', or to put it another way, each syllable of 'river' is half the single syllable of 'lake'. After they have practiced, they can mix up the words in a pattern but keep to the same beat. You might have 'lake, lake, river, river, lake, river, lake, lake' or 'river, lake, river, lake, river, river, lake river'. If children have difficulty keeping to the beat they can clap as they say each word. Keeping to eight beats will be useful later when introducing conventional musical notation. However, a project could swing along without becoming a technical musical exercise. Look forward for ideas about a less structured approach.

The word 'river' is in effect a pair of quavers ♫ and the word 'lake' a crochet ♩. When the children are comfortable with chanting together and have made up a number of different patterns, they can try splitting into two or more groups and testing the effect of overlaying the rhythms one on another. For example, one group could be chanting 'lake, lake, lake, lake', whilst another is chanting 'river, lake, river, lake' to the same clapped beat at the same time. When they are all in time ask them to stop the clapping so they can hear the effect of the overlaid voices.

The possibilities build from here. The children could take a phrase from their story. For example, 'we went to sea in a boat'. This could be organised into a simple, rhythm 'we, went, to sea, in, a, boat'.

Or, by extending the last 'boat' sound to two beats it could be:

Three syllable words or phrase, for example, 'motor boat', could become triplets. The chant could be also notated visually with simple pictures and words, repeated as the chant dictates. In effect, the children can create visual patterns to represent their rhythmic chants. Having the conventional notation alongside becomes a fast way of introducing this to the class. Phrases that are more complicated can be added and overlaid. However, the more complex and layered chants will only work if the children keep to the same underlying beat.

Why not use a grid to show several patterns of sounds look when written or drawn? This will be useful to show the children what is happening when they attempt to overlay the different rhythms together. However, children should experiment with the sounds before attempting to understand or decipher notation. They can always tape record their work to help them remember their different ideas.

we went to	sea	in a	boat
the	sea	was	rough
rough	rough	rough	rough
In a boat	In a boat	In a boat	In a boat

Children can compose their own rhythms using words and phrases from their communities (or the more conventional notation if they are happy with it). When they have created their rhythms, they might be able to change the pitch of the notes so that they make a melody and even harmonies. For example, in the grid on the previous page the 'rough' sounds could all be played at one pitch, the 'in a boat' phrase could be an ascending triplet. Read the variation on this project that follows for ideas about how to create a simple melody. The top line, 'we, went to sea, in a, boat', could become a simple melodic line. Dynamics, degrees of loudness and softness, can also be introduced to each part. Adding a sense of phrasing by emphasis on one or more beats as well as dynamics can create quite a complicated sound.

It would not be too difficult to find ways of making these chants semi-naturalistic, mimicking the pulse of the sea or the regular beat of men quarrying stone, just to take two examples.

The approach to creating a rhythmic chant and the possibility of developing this simple idea towards musical composition is quite formal. Here is a less formal approach, which has the advantage of allowing children to be more expressive but the disadvantage of missing opportunities to teach them about music.

With the whole class together, find examples of different sentences and phrases from the imaginary myths or legends. For example, 'we make tiny boats with candles in; we sail them down the river'. Say or chant the phrases one at a time, experimenting with emphasising different elements. For example, in the second phrase, 'we sail them down the river' the words 'sail' 'down' and 'river' could be chanted more slowly, even languidly, to suggest the slow moving water. Beat out a rhythm, until you find a natural fit to the words and the whole class can practise the chant. Try some variations until everyone seems to feel the chant sounds right.

Use a xylophone or glockenspiel with some notes removed to make a pentatonic scale (CDEGA or use the black notes on a keyboard). Ask a child to experiment with any three notes at random. Play these one after another, repeating some. Now fit the notes to the first line of the chant. Repeat this with the second line. More notes will create a more complex melody.

We make ti - ny boats with cand - les in; we sail them down the ri - ver.

Now the children can practise the rhythmic chant with the different notes, creating a simple melodic line. You can go on to add dynamics (loudness and softness) and emphasis (phrasing) as above. This is the start of a simple song.

Can the children find ways of suggesting the general mood of their community using rhythm, dynamics, the notes or the phrasing? This is expression. For example, a community that sees themselves as strong, powerful workers who mine for gold and live under a volcano will be likely to have a song that suggests power; a community that spends time on a sunny beach by a gentle sea may want to try and create something of this atmosphere.

After the whole class has created a simple song with the teacher, ask children to work in their communities to see if they can create a chant, add the three notes to make a melody, and go on to add dynamics and phrasing. Able children could use this technique to compose a verse or chorus from a song on their own. Less able children will need more adult support.

Whichever teaching strategy is used, from this section or from other advice about teaching music in primary schools, the aim is that each of the imaginative communities uses ideas, springing from their embryonic spoken and written culture, to create their music. This music, even if this is only a simple rhythmic chant, belongs to them, and its character and meaning has been created by themselves out ideas that they own. »147

Movement into dance

Photo Roy Campbell-Moore, Diversions dance project, Cardiff

This project continues to build on the children's growing cultural experiences as members of their imaginary communities. However, it is worth a reminder that the route to this point does not need to include every activity described up to now. Neither is the order of the activities in the book fixed. Teachers may swap activities around – look in parts 2 and 3 of the book – before deciding to bring movement and dance into play. It is possible to look back to the section on creating an imaginary island and creating a community for inspiration for this project. Why not consider movement as the very first way that children express ideas? The movements could then become the springboard for creating myths, legends and story strips.

First, children will need to warm up. There are many different ways to do this but why not invent an exercise linked to the island? For example:

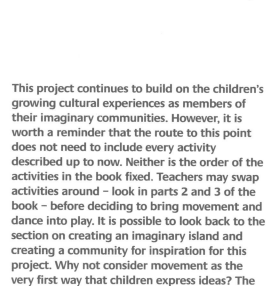

There is only one way to cross the river north of Malexa, the inhabitants of the island have to wade across and the water reaches all the way up to their necks. The problem is that leeches latch on to all parts of the body. People have learnt that the best way of getting rid of these pesky beasts is to concentrate on each part of the body in turn. First shake your left hand, slowly at first and then faster and faster. Imagine you are trying to shake off a leech! Now shake your right hand, slowly then quickly, now your left arm and then the right. Now the left foot, now the right foot...

Children can bit by bit shake every part of the body until at the end they have to shake all over. Its only then that all the leeches have gone.

Ask the children to stay in their groups. Ask children about some of the different things they do in the community. Perhaps, they swim, fish, milk cows, work in the docks unloading boxes, dig for gold or pick cherries? There will be many ideas. Invite the children to try miming one of the movements that go with the activities they have suggested. Ask them to exaggerate each movement, enacting it slowly, so that every one can see clearly each part of the action. Repeat this with each group so that the whole class can see each group inventing a movement.

Now ask the all the groups to practise their chosen movement, moving slowly and clearly emphasising each part. Can they make the movement in unison? Maybe one child could act as a leader, so that other children can follow his pace. Each community can now perform their movement in unison for the whole class repeating it again and again.

A teacher could introduce ideas designed to increase children's understanding of a range of possible components of movement. For example, children could explore the differences between activity, stillness, extending outwards, contracting inwards, rotating, moving in a direction, moving away, moving towards, creating a support, leaving the ground and balancing. Each of these ideas can apply to the whole body or to part of the body. Each individual idea can be further unpacked. For example, 'contracting

inwards' could include making a ball, curling, crouching, shoulders hunched, closing a hand, head between the knees. The same notions could become emotional: cowering, hiding, lost, sheltering, sad, inward looking.

The point will be reached where the children can see how to create meaningful movements themselves. When the preparation is sufficient for the teaching strategy you are using, challenge the children to create two or three more movements, each showing an element of their life in their community. These can be linked together to form a simple dance. The children could also go back to their story strips and invent movements for each stage of the myth or legend; these could be quite expressive if they begin to associate movements with emotions as hinted at above. A third possibility is to link the movements to the rhythms and songs they may have created (see page 51); or to turn the idea around, use the less formal method of creating a rhythm, but take the cue from the movements rather than sentences or phrases. For example, ask the children to clap out a rhythm that will fit their movements. You can see how it is possible for the children to create a dance with music, providing the structure set by the teacher is able to both take them one step at a time through the process and at the same time open up a space for them to express their own ideas.

1.5 Designing for the home

Cultural identity is expressed through the design of objects which make up part of our daily lives. The children will be able enrich their imaginary cultures by designing for the home. The projects that follow include: tableware, textiles and fabric design and clothes and fashion design.

The inspiration for the designs will be found in the creation of the imaginary communities. The design of each item is another way the imaginary communities can express their uniqueness. In Part 1 of this book we have focused on an imaginary island but as we have seen teachers could generate similar project structures with other themes such as an imaginary world or an imaginary city with different neighbourhoods or boroughs (look back a page 33). Children may have created a myth or legend, developed an oral tradition and been involved in music and dance. Each of these activities may suggest ideas for designs, although the most useful activities to precede this section are found on pages 35 and 36. These are about creating patterns and motifs.

Teachers and children are unlikely to have time for all the projects described here, but the starting point for each is the same. Gather the class together and ask:

'I would like each community to remind us all about what you have created up to now. To help you remember as much as possible think about each of these questions in turn:

Where is your community? What is it like? What happens in and around your community? What kinds of things do you do? Is there anything special about your community? Have you designed or drawn anything for your community? Are there any stories? Are there any songs, chants or dances?'

Ask the children to gather together any relevant visual work, particularly on pattern and motifs, but including any story strips and cartoons. Their ideas will all feed into the projects that follow.

Teachers could look forward to other parts of this book. For example, designs could inspired by abstraction, dreams, and animals; or by an imaginary beliefs or the need to commemorate an event.

Decorating tableware

Invite children to create some draft designs on paper plates. Use the non-waxy variety that will take felt pen, pastel or paint. Children could use the plates as templates to cut circles of paper to use as roughs to try out ideas. They should work in their community groups, but each child could design their own plate. Look for circular objects that are smaller than the diameter of the paper plate that could be useful for drawing circles inside the main form. The children could also divide the circle into segments. Look back at the section on pattern and motifs for ideas about making and using smaller templates to repeat parts of a pattern. Ask children to think about the background colour. Do they want their plate to be white?

The children can go on to make a plate from a clay slab. But schools can also buy bisque ware (biscuit ware) which is plain, once fired and unglazed ware, which children can decorate. This can be surprisingly inexpensive. An Internet search will throw up a number of suppliers. One advantage is that schools could buy a variety of bisque tableware, including dessert bowls, dinner plates, side plates, soup bowls, mugs, cups and saucers. Perhaps each community could collaborate to create a set, with each child contributing by decorating one of the different items. The designs could have elements in common to the community (a shared motif, pattern and colours) and elements that are individual to the maker.

Children can simply use acrylic paints to apply the designs and special ceramic paint is also available, but likely to be expensive. If you have access to a kiln ask the bisque supplier to recommend a paint-on glaze. Many glazes are now completely safe and can be used in schools. The children's glaze decorated bisque plates can then be fired to fix the designs. If children are to paint on the plate, they will need to be able to outline their design lightly before they start painting. Rather than use pencils ask children to use a very pale colour or white and a very thin tipped brush to draw in paint on the plate. This has two advantages. First, children can not be expected to show an exaggerated amount of detail on the ceramic ware. Second, the very pale lines can be easily covered over as the children add colour. This hides mistakes and offers the opportunity to have bold blocks of colour. Some plate designs will be improved by strong outlines. The pale guidelines are the template for these. **»147**

Textiles and fabric designs

We can introduce children to a number of different techniques that can be used for designing fabrics. In this section we will touch on weaving, block printing, cold-water paste batik and screen-printing. The screen-printing project is an example of how the imaginary islands project could be enhanced by working with professional artists who bring their skills into school to help realise children's design ideas.

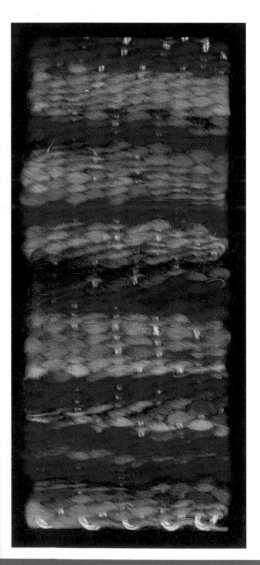

Weaving

Weaving is essentially the combination of two threads. The lengthwise thread, which is attached to the loom, is called the warp. The thread woven across and often carried by a shuttle is called the weft. The loom is a piece of equipment, which helps the weaver to combine these two sets of threads. »148

The simplest form of weaving in school is paper weaving. You can also use strips of card, plastic, or anything else that can be woven, by passing the weft in and out of the warp in various ways. Coloured paper is an ideal way for pupils to experiment with different types of weave as the pattern can easily be seen. When pupils understand the basics of weaving, projects can be undertaken using simple card looms and wool. The card holds the warp threads whilst the weft is woven under and over warp with various combinations of colours and patterns.

Larger weavings can be made using strips of offcut fabrics and larger strips of coloured plastics, in fact anything that can be woven. Hazel and willow stems (withies) can be woven to create outdoor structures. You could think laterally about how to make a large loom. For example, use a little used doorway. Screw a series of hooks into the underside of the top of the doorframe. Use coloured string, a natural fibre, or thick, strong wool to create a warp. The bottom of the warp threads are attached to hooks screwed into a robust plank that is the exact width of the door. The plank sits on the floor inside the doorway and the weight of the wood helps to tension the warp. The gaps between the warp threads need to be big enough for the children to easily weave the fabric strips. After the children have finished the weaving, take it down carefully and use strong carpet or fabric tape on the reverse side to hold the loose warp and weft in place; trim to make a finished looking product. After introducing children to the techniques and before they go on to make a weaving ask:

What kinds of things do you think you could make from the weaving techniques I have shown you? Rugs? Wall hangings? Place mats? Something for a ceremony?
If you were more skilled and we had better equipment and more time, what do you think could be woven?
How do you think fabrics for clothes are woven?

This is an opportunity to introduce children to commercially woven fabrics. Ask them to use a magnifying glass or microscope to see if they can spot the warp and the weft threads. Why not use a digital microscope and print out various images of the detail of different woven fabrics? Search the Internet to find more information about woven structures. Crucially, show children examples of woven fabrics from other cultures, at least in illustration. Look back at page 38. The example of weavers from Guatemala is a good illustration of what can be researched and shown to children. Identify the different kinds of threads that could be used like cotton, wool and silk. Talk about where the threads come from and what they are made of. If possible visit a mill or invite a weaver into school. Make a display all about weaving.

When the children weave an object for their particular imaginary culture, they will have seen how our own as well as other societies and cultures use weaving to make important items in use every day, not least fabrics for clothes. This is another brief example of how the imaginary island theme might end in a series of activities that focus on a particular process and related skills. Although the project here has taken a path to become more process-orientated, the crucial lesson is that weaving has purpose and that woven items have a part to play in the expression of every culture. An interesting example from the United Kingdom is the significance of woven tartans to Scottish clans.

Block printing

Printed fabrics are used extensively in clothing and furnishings. You could make a collection of commercially printed fabrics to show the children. Bring in examples from home and use a digital camera to record furnishings. There are many examples of printed fabrics from different parts of the world on the Internet. Before this project gets underway revisit the imaginary island and ask the children to imagine how printed fabrics could be used in their imaginary island community?

What items of clothing could you make with a printed fabric? Where could you use printed fabrics in the home? Where could you use printed fabrics in the town or village? Have you any unusual ideas about how you could use printed fabric?

I am going to show you one way of printing a sheet of fabric using printing blocks. You will then be able to design a pattern to print using several blocks with different colours, shapes and motifs. You will be able to repeat these again and again to make a pattern.

After revisiting the pattern project (page 36) children can use simple shapes to make a relief-printing block. Each block can be inked up and printed onto fabric many times, so that the motif or element of the pattern is repeated again and again on the fabric. **»148**

Look out for African and Asian wooden fabric printing blocks. Sometimes these can be purchased to use in schools. Check the Internet – there is plenty of information and images about block printing on fabric, particularly from Africa and Asia. A search using the term 'block printing on fabric' will offer links to India and Africa. For something more specific, try looking for Adinkra textiles (African cloth printing tradition of pre-colonial origin) from the Ashanti kingdom of Ghana.

There are many other tools and materials that could be adapted to printing onto fabric. Children could experiment making printing blocks with leaves, string and drawing pins (try pinning drawing pins into a block in different designs and printing the resulting pattern). Sponges, plastic play shapes for toddlers and much else besides could all be used to make prints and patterns.

Cold water and flour paste resist

As with all the processes outlined in this section, designs and ideas are generated by the imaginary islands project. The children can plan how they can decorate their fabrics using motifs, patterns and images and ideas from myths, stories and cartoons. Teachers could also consider using ideas from parts 2 and 3 of this book as starting points for design ideas that could be used in this process.

Cold water flour paste resist is a simple form of batik. The flour and water paste is poured or squeezed on to the fabric to form shapes and lines of a design. When the paste is dry, children can add colour using fabric paints and sponges or paintbrushes. They fill in the areas defined by the paste lines.

Each child in the group can contribute ideas towards a final piece of fabric. Look back at page 35 and at page 36. This project will mean so much more if children can clearly see why they are decorating fabric, what fabrics might be used for and why their images, motifs and patterns look the way they do. The photographs on this page show children at work on the various stages of the process.

You could take this opportunity to show children fabrics from different cultures that are coloured with the batik process. This usually involves wax and dying. There is a great deal of information and many images to be found on the Internet. »149

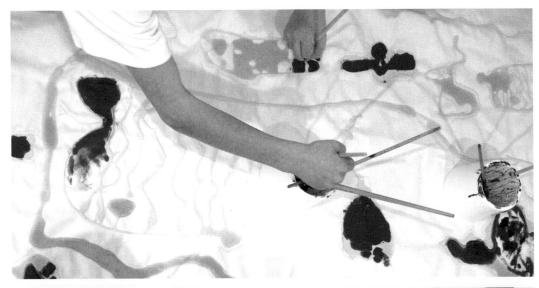

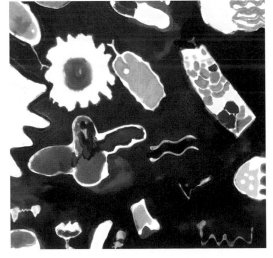

Mono printing

The beauty of mono printing is that it involves a very direct way of creating images. In its simplest form children simply draw their ideas into ink or paint rolled out onto a smooth, non-absorbent surface like thick acetate, plastic sheet or Perspex. You could also work directly onto a smooth tabletop or the surface of something like the door of a kitchen unit. Children can use their fingers, brushes, sponges, in fact anything that will make a mark. In this form of mono printing, the idea is that they are removing colour, so it is a kind of negative process to normal painting and drawing. It is the paler lines and marks that are left after children have, say, dragged their finger through the ink that will make the image. Mono-prints can be made onto any surface that will accept the ink or paint, including paper card and fabric. One way to mono-print onto fabric is to first make the image. Next, ask four children to each hold a corner of a piece of fabric stretching it taut. They should lower this onto the inky surface keeping the tension so that the fabric does not crease or fold. Apply a little pressure with a clean roller or the palm of a hand, gently smoothing the fabric over the ink. Peel the fabric off the surface to reveal the image. Practise first with the paint, ink, fabric and printing surface you are going to use, as no two sets of circumstances are the same. Even the heat or relative humidity in the classroom will affect the outcome. **»149**

Screen-printing

Screen-printing involves a higher level of specialist knowledge, materials and equipment than is usually found in primary schools. This project is an example of a county wide project where a small team of artists were invited to tour schools within a local authority and create banners from fabrics. They used screen printing, bringing all the materials and equipment with them into school. They worked with ideas linked to the imaginary island theme. Some of the images were photographed and reproduced digitally onto weatherproof plastics to hang in the city as part of a major cultural celebration. Working in this way, linking communities of schools into one project which, is itself part of a real county wide event, really helps to emphasise the layering of culture. The children's imaginary communities on imaginary islands became seen as part of a larger cultural group that stretched across a city. In this case, community artists (and artists who work in schools) became part of developing both the children's imaginary cultures, as well as the school and the whole city culture during the celebration. In the project neither the children nor their teachers had, and were not expected to have, the technical skills needed to make the screen prints on their own. The adult artists directed the process and the children where able to help, learning how their visual ideas are transformed through a process into a product. »149

To make a screen print a special ink is applied onto a screen, this is a porous, mesh-like fabric. A squeegee is pulled or pushed, drawing the ink across the porous material of the screen and so squashing it through the many tiny holes onto the fabric beneath. The design is made by blocking the holes with some kind of template or stencil. The simplest templates are cardboard or paper shapes. These shapes then appear on the fabric beneath as blanks, no ink has been allowed through the screen where the template was placed. The process can be repeated several times building up more complex coloured images. Commercial screen-printing creates a screen using photographic techniques and light sensitive material to block the holes of the mesh. This allows very subtle and sophisticated images with very high resolutions to be printed. Many printed fabrics as well as cardboard and plastic packaging are produced by commercial screen-printing techniques.

Photo: Geraldine Deayton

Clothing and fashion design

These beads are for Speaceal accaition like Festivals

This Designer Top is made of the Finest bush leaves

This gorgeus Skirt is made of the 3 ftar leaves.

These wonerful Clogs are made of Fine wood by the woodland teams.

Here is an example of starting a project without reference to the imaginary island theme, which runs through this part of the book. However, designing clothes that people wear in the island's towns and village could easily spin off from earlier activities. For example, look back at page 30. This project could follow on from the creating communities activity. However, the following approach asks the children to create ideas about imaginary human beings from scratch.

You are going to create some imaginary human beings. Each group in the class will create a different kind of imaginary people. I am going to ask you to work together and answer each of the questions on these sheets. Choose someone in the group to be the secretary and he or she will note down in rough the ideas you come up with. Talk about one question at a time.

Children could use brainstorming, word lists or a mind-mapping technique. If you think that the children will find the activity difficult, create an example human with the whole class first. You could also create a tighter structure for the children to follow by sub-dividing each section. For example, the first question about what the imaginary people might look like in the list that follows, could sub-divide into decisions about hair, skin, height, eye colour, distinguishing features and so on. You could provide a list of examples for the second question about where imaginary people might live such as houses, trees, villages, by rivers, in high rise towers, and ask children to describe in more detail what their chosen place is like. Why not see what they create first and ask them to go back and add more detail if you feel their ideas are a little thin?

What do the imaginary people look like?
Where do they live?
How do they behave?
What do they wear?
How do they communicate?
What do they like?
What do they do?
What are they called?

Of course, there are immediate opportunities to draw these imaginary people. This could make an excellent activity for the sketchbook or perhaps children could work on a larger sheet that they could fill with smaller visual and written ideas. One group could prepare one sheet with each child contributing some drawings or notes. Ask the children to use these sheets as prompts to help them prepare and relate oral descriptions of their imaginary people to the whole class.

Talking and sharing ideas about the imaginary people will help to cement the children's identification with what they have created. If the children have worked on large sheets of paper, try asking them to use these as prompts to help describe their imaginary people to the whole class. Ideas can be both visual and written; the combination is very powerful, as any expert on preparing presentations in business and industry will confirm. This is a useful skill to develop and ways of presenting a brand new idea, in this case about people, can be practised using both words and pictures.

The teacher can now ask children to think about what these people wear. Again, talking about all the different kinds of clothes will help remind children about the enormous variety of hats, scarves, shoes, belts, overcoats, gloves, shirts, tunics, gowns, dresses, tops, ponchos, kilts, and socks... (all these and much more are possible). One variation in the preparation would be to provide the children with descriptions of real people who live in very different circumstances in different parts of the world. For example, compare the Inuit people with a Polynesian Islander. One obvious way that cultures of all sizes and types express their identity is through the clothes they wear. Contrast, for a moment, the different dress sense of a Guatemalan of Mayan descent, a Californian surfer, a nun, a London banker and a courtier to Louis XIV! The children only listen to descriptions, do not see the people in advance and have to design clothing they think they might wear. The children's designs can be compared with photographs of clothing worn by the people you introduced and described.

Using templates to design clothes

Encouraging children to use templates when teaching art has often been frowned on in polite art education circles. Perhaps it is because templates are just too easy or simply do not appear to be creative enough. Worse, perhaps the children are somehow cheating! The truth is, of course, that templates are just one of many tools and aids that artists and designers have always used and from time to time children will find them helpful too. In the project illustrated here they help to short cut difficult technical problems associated with drawing figures so that children can work with confidence on the project theme, which is about designing clothes.

In this project, children are asked to imagine what kind of clothes the imaginary people they have created would wear. For example, this might depend on where they lived (in a hot or a cold climate for example), what they liked to do, what they had to do to survive, what they believed. Is it better to wear bright or sombre clothes? This project can also be linked to other parts of the book. For example, look forward to ideas about creating personalities, or look forward to Part 3 of the book for more ideas about linking to beliefs.

Give the children A4 templates of the human figure copied from a book of fashion templates especially designed for students studying the early stages of fashion design. You can also find free figure templates to download from the Internet. These are usually simple, boldly outlined standing figures that appear to be wearing underwear. You can also find templates for children's figures. Ask the children to place thin A4 copier paper over the A4 template. They will just be able to see the outline of the figure underneath their paper. Next, ask them to draw their ideas for the clothing, as though they were imagining dressing their figure, but without drawing the underlying body shape defined by the template. They simply draw the clothes. The only exception is when they need to draw parts of arms, legs, hands and any other bare skin that is showing; in this case, they can copy the shapes of the body template they can see through their paper. This technique allows children to focus on the clothing designs. They are less likely to be thrown off track by the very difficult problem of drawing figures in proportion and so becoming very dissatisfied with how their drawings look.

The children can also make their own templates. Collect a wide selection of suitable magazine and newspaper photographs of figures – include different children and adults. The children can select the figures they would like to use for the templates. There is no need to cut out the figures accurately. To strengthen the photograph it might be best to use a glue stick to glue it onto some thicker paper or thin card. Next, use a bold marker pen to over draw a basic outline on the shape of the figure that the children imagine is underneath the clothing on the photograph. Again, although this needs to be done carefully, there is no need to show any detail. Place a sheet of thin white paper over the emboldened image and ask children to draw the outline shape. They need to end up with a simple boldly outlined figure on white paper. This becomes their template and is used in the same way as above.

The dress, Shoes, Bag and hat are all made from Shells

To recap, if you have read the sections that make up Part 1 of this book, you will have seen how a teacher might structure a wider project that has the creation of an imaginary island at its heart. Other broad themes that could work in a very similar way include imaginary worlds and imaginary cities. Children have worked together to build an embryonic imaginary culture, a kind of faux culture, by first creating communities (in this case settlements, villages or towns), in which the imaginary inhabitants could make art and design, create myths and legends, tell stories and create music and dance. The art has focused on imaginative narrative drawings and designing for the home. Teachers can also incorporate elements from Parts 2 and 3 of this book. For example, children might create an imaginary system of beliefs or an imaginary political party for their community, or they might look inwards towards individuals by considering how they could express ideas about imaginary personalities. The overarching principle is that children are creating meanings. Expression through the arts is part of communicating those meanings and thus children are creating culture.

Public events are central to any society and an important part of cultural expression. Suitable events could include celebrations, festivals, carnivals, parties, birthdays, anniversaries, commemorations, funerals, weddings and religious ceremonies. The communities on the children's imaginary island could also experience important public events. How could teachers help children create ideas for an imaginary event?

1.6
Celebrating culture

Creating an event

You could start this process by introducing the idea of significant events where many people come together to do something special. What happens when someone has a birthday? What happens when two people want to get married? What happens when someone dies? Are there special times of year when people celebrate together? What happens in a place of worship like a church, a temple or a mosque? A teacher could research examples of different festivals and carnivals in different parts of the world, show children images and tell the story behind the event.

Now ask children to brainstorm or mind-map all the different possible events that could take place in their community. Each community should choose one idea for an event. Why are the events happening? What happens at the event? There is more mind-mapping or brainstorming as the children share ideas. This exploration could become quite detailed and lead to more oral or written work. Perhaps a child could imagine what a reporter would say in a newspaper or on television when reporting on the imaginary event.

In this section, there are ideas about making body adornments, masks and carnival puppets. Teachers may wish to control the outcomes more tightly to take advantage of work already completed. For example, the children may have already created chants, songs or dances. These could be used now.

Photo: Geraldine Deayton

Costume and body adornment

What could children make that could be worn at the event? You might think of headwear, jewellery, cloaks and capes, belts, chains and medallions, arm and leg protectors. A glance through images of events in different cultures around the world will generate a host of ideas. Teachers could also explore face painting and body art. The following project uses the simple materials and techniques to create elements of a costume for the imaginary event.

Remind children about work they may have already completed on creating motifs and patterns. Look back at page 35 and page 36 for ideas. Show children the tools and materials that they will use. In this simplest of projects, these divide into the following categories:

- Paper and card, including scrap card from packaging.
- Materials that can be used for joining, fastening or attaching two pieces of paper or card, this includes string, tape, glue, a stapler, treasury tags, paper fasteners, wool, pipe cleaners, ribbon, narrow strips of off cut fabric and wire.
- Tools for cutting, including scissors, hole punches, and, under supervision, craft knives.
- Materials for graphic decoration, which could include oil pastels, felt pens, marker pens, wax crayons and paint.
- Materials for collaged decoration, including metallic papers, feathers, leaves, shells, pre-cut coloured shapes, photographs and photocopies of relevant images and art work, computer printouts of designs children have created digitally and anything else you could imagine might be useful. For example, one group found that they could create a tunic like garment with strips of artificial grass!

Structure a number of short activities to allow children to experiment, finding out the different ways the basic shapes of cardboard and paper could be joined and attached. You may need to show them some techniques they may not think of themselves. For example, punching holes with the hole punch and using any of the strips and lengths of material to join or hang one shape to or from another. Making a slit or slot in a sheet of card means another piece just a little narrower than the slot can be passed through it. Paper or thin card can be rolled and glued to form a tube. The long tubes can be sliced to make rings and smaller tubes of varying lengths. These can be strung together. Paper can be joined by folding one strip into another. Paper fasteners create rivet like effects. It is best to find the time to experiment yourself, before the lesson, to explore in your own way just how the

various tools and materials can be used to combine, join and attach.

Now, ask the children to create the components of the costume they want to make. Children should work together in their community groups. If time is limited, each community could create one costume. Each child contributes work towards some element of the costume, although they will need to collaborate on the more complex bits. There are four main parts to the work:

- Cutting the basic shapes and components.
- Decorating and colouring these components (which in some cases is better done before they are cut).
- Joining and attaching the pieces in different ways.
- Assembling the finished costume on a model and adding final details.

Designing in advance of making is a possibility, although, unless children can experience the problems and limitations of the making before they design, they may be too ambitious in their design ideas. Children might work more fluently and with greater inventiveness once they have had a chance to find out something of the possibilities of the different tools and materials you have collected for them. However, this project could be linked to ideas about designing clothing.

If the children printed fabrics (see page 57), they could use these as part of their costume. Simple headbands can be made with pattern strips drawn onto thin card created as part of the pattern project (see page 36). Two holes are punched on each side of the strip, which is tightened around the head with string or wool. Face and body painting could be part of the final 'look'.

You should not overlook the possibility of using printouts of digital images and designs either created on the computer or photographed with a digital camera. Digital images can be further manipulated with simple to use effects tools in photo software. These printouts can be cut and collaged onto various card shapes, or rolled to make tubes (see above). For more ideas about creating and manipulating images look forward to page 97 for advice about using a photocopier.

Record the results with a digital camera for display; in the flurry of excitement that this kind of project creates, it is easy to overlook detail and the small achievements of individual pupils.

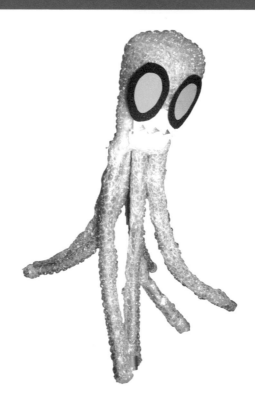

Making masks and carnival puppets

There is much practical advice on mask making available in publications and on the Internet. However, what these 'how to make it' guides rarely do, is show how the activity of mask making can carry meaning. Clearly, the expressive quality of masks can be highly significant. For example, the ability to change the wearer's identity to signify something other than human, is one reason why masks are used in spiritual ceremonies in many different cultures.

If the children are planning an event, they could decide that masks would help them tell a story or change character. A mask might signify an animal, a god or an emotion. For example, if you look back at the story strips (see page 44) and the subsequent pages about creating an oral tradition, masks could be used to help tell a myth or a legend.

Examples of masks from many different cultures are not difficult to find. At the time of writing, in November 2005, there is even a web site called masksoftheworld.com, which not only contains an enormous number of images, but also has explanations on the significance and use of each mask. Such a site is typical of the way the Internet has made visual and textual research on cultures so available to teachers.

One of the easiest of all mask-making techniques can be used. Children are going to make a stick mask – a mask held on a stick in front of the face. This technique is also relevant for the project that follows.

The basic idea is that the simple shape of the mask is cut out of card. This needs to be stiff enough not to collapse or bend in on itself. If you do use thin card, which children can cut out themselves, then find a way of strengthening the simple shapes using strips of thicker card glued onto the reverse. A stick, perhaps a length of dowel, is fixed centrally to the back of the mask with plenty of tape. This needs to be roughly the right length so that the child can comfortably hold it in front of her face. The card shape is then coloured and decorated. The card mask can be folded to create a more three-dimensional effect.

For example, an elongated man's head shape will look more interesting if the mask is scored lightly down the long centre and the folded in slightly; the stick is fixed in the central 'v' fold.

The first part of the project is for children to work out, in their community groups, what masks would be useful in the final event or performance. Second, they could explore different kinds of outline shapes that could be used to create the mask. For example, if they want a lion mask, could they find examples of lion's heads and collect the simple outline to use as inspiration for the mask. Masks could easily refer to any fish, insect, mammal or bird. If the children want to create a character based on a human head, it will be useful if they can see examples of how exaggeration can be used to give the mask character. For example, a head mask might be excessively long, have huge ears, or an extraordinary pointed chin, or a very wide round forehead. Children could practise a number of shapes before deciding which one will be used for the mask.

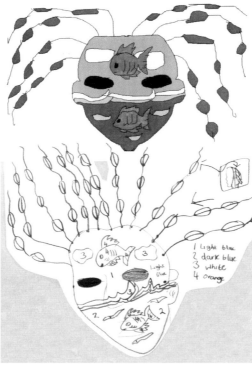

Next the children will cut out their mask and create a design for it that reflects the character they have chosen to represent or enact during the performance. The whole of the mask could be covered in colour, lines, shapes and patterns. Because the masks are about imaginary characters, they do not need to be realistic. This can help give confidence to children who find drawing more difficult. The big challenge is can they create expressions, colours and designs that express something significant about the content of the event or performance? A look at different masks from different cultures will help.

The final phase is to add any extra adornments or decorations before making any additional folds and taping on the dowel stick. Look back at the previous section about making costume and body adornments. The same making practices used there can be applied to the masks. Children can attach, hang and collage any number of objects, shapes and even images to the mask.

A very similar technique can be used to make carnival puppets. Just as with masks, numerous publications and web sites offer advice on making puppets and puppetry. Some of the more practical and accessible techniques in primary school include stick puppets, finger puppets and glove puppets.

The carnival puppets for this project are simply larger versions of stick puppets and are not difficult to make. They are really just flat shapes cut from card connected to each other in a flexible way. One carnival scale puppet can be an impressive part of an event or performance. Perhaps there could be one large puppet to represent the whole island? Perhaps each community could construct a puppet of their own.

The puppet is made in different sections. The idea is that a child holds up each section on a stick. For example, a dragon puppet could be divided into five parts: a head and neck, a body, two wings and a tail. Each part is controlled by a stick, which the child can move up and down or from side to side. The parts are connected in a way that allows movement. For example, the head is a decorated cardboard shape of a dragon's head, which is connected to the body by strips of red material. A stick is attached to the back of the cardboard shape. This allows the child holding the head to create quite animated and expressive movements with the stick. The wings could be attached to the body with shorter strips of cloth or canvas. This gives a limited amount of movement to the two children controlling each wing. Just as in the mask project each shape can be coloured and decorated with any combination of techniques. »149

Performance – celebrating culture

How can we help children share all their ideas about the culture of their imaginary community? The outcomes from Part 1 that could be included in a celebration or performance are:

- Illustrated imaginary island map drawings
- Oral and written work about imaginary communities
- Motifs
- Pattern designs
- Imaginary myths, legends or stories
- Drawn story strips
- Video clips of children presenting their story to camera
- Comic pages
- Animation
- Rhythms and chants
- Songs
- Dance
- Designed tableware
- Weavings
- Printed fabrics
- Fabrics decorated with a cold water paste batik technique
- Imaginary people
- Designs for clothes
- Costumes, jewellery and body adornments
- Masks
- Puppets
- A performance

More outcomes could be generated and interlinked with this work by introducing ideas from Parts 2 and 3. For example:

- Portraits of the island inhabitants
- Imaginary personalities and characters
- Paintings and collages created from ideas generated by stories or dreams
- Imaginary animals (part of island folklore)
- Imaginary machines (that do practical or magical tasks linked to real life or made-up stories)
- Greetings cards
- Imaginary belief systems
- Places of worship either designed or constructed
- Installations
- An imaginary political party, complete with logos, election posters and manifestos
- Videoed television interviews
- All kinds of ways of investigating the imaginary environment
- Art for the imaginary community, including sculpture for specific sites

These lists are not in any way exhaustive, but they do show how teachers could pick a number of projects, which when taught in the context of the creation of an imaginary island community, could come together form part of a celebration of an imaginary culture. The images in this section were taken at the Illuzia imaginary island project at the Wales Millennium Centre with teachers and children from Cardiff schools. »149

In conclusion, the thesis is that when children work in this way, they are creating meaning that they own. They identify strongly with what they are making and see the sense of it. Moreover, they can see how cultural expression develops as people create art that expresses who they are and what they believe. This art reflects the circumstances of people's lives. As the imaginary culture develops it becomes self-generating as one outcome leads to ideas about others. This offers teachers opportunities to show children adult art, craft and design from different cultures. Children can more easily identify with the reasons why the art was made and the reasons it looks the way it does. They more readily identify with the people who made it. They will gradually understand and respect more about their own and other cultures.

There is limited time and opportunity to teach the arts in primary schools so inevitably teachers will need to fashion projects that fit the practical circumstances. But at the end of the day, if you like this approach and have organised some of the projects on, say, the imaginary island theme, children will have the opportunity to share their imaginary culture with other children in the class or school. Planning a performance or presentation for adults will also motivate children. Rather than a simple performance for assembly, consider asking the children to organise an event for an important visitor to their community. Their task is to explain everything about their lives and to show their culture through the various arts outcomes they have created during the extended project. This offers more fascinating possibilities to see how the different groups in the same class can create very different outcomes from the same teaching input. Here is a list of possible ideas for presenting the cultures:

- Performances that bring together the music, rhythm, dance, costume, mask and puppet projects.
- Exhibitions that show off the art craft and design work in the context of the island.
- Video (in effect television) that takes the viewer on a tour of the project and includes presentations to camera and interviews with the islanders.
- A book that includes accounts, stories, comic book pages and illustrations from each community

- Recordings (in effect radio) that include oral descriptions of life in the communities and stories.
- A computer presentation where children use digital images, photographs and video of their work to tell others about their community.
- A parallel presentation or performance of ideas from real world cultures.

This section is a collection of ideas that may suggest links to the children's own art work inspired by their imaginary island communities. Apart from the African fable 'The King's Magic Drum', one good source for images and ideas has been chosen – the Compass on-line database at the British Museum (www.thebritishmuseum.ac.uk). If you want to find more detailed information about each image, simply search the Compass database using key words from the image title. The examples in this section are only indicative of what teachers could find and use and are not intended to be prescriptive. There are legions of web sites offering links to different cultures and societies both historical and modern with images that can be saved to show children and text to help the teacher contextualise the art and artefacts. To cite one non-visual example, in the Pacific Islands, stories are passed on orally from generation to generation. You could find stories on the Internet from French Polynesia, the Hawaiian Islands, Kiribati, Mangareva, the Marquesas Islands, Samoa, Tahiti, Tahuata, Tonga, and Tuamotu. Find the islands on a globe or a map. Research something about the lives of the islanders. Talk about the geography and climate. Discuss problems that islanders may have and the advantages and disadvantages of living there. Revisit the children's own stories, myths and legends, and talk about the characteristics of their own imaginary island communities.

1.7
Introducing different cultures

The argument here is that it is after the children have had the experience of creating their own cultural expressions that they are more interested in, and better able to understand, the context in which other people, from different parts of the world, create art, craft and design. Although it can never be a hard and fast rule, the advice in this book suggests that it is often best to show children adult art after, rather than before, they make their own art. The premise is that children understand more about what the art means and appreciate more about the people who made it, after they have been involved in the process of creating cultural meaning themselves. This approach also prevents adult images and ideas from becoming too dominant an influence. The danger is that children might produce meaningless pastiches of the way other art looks with no reference to its significance, if they are overwhelmed by the adult art they are shown. Having said that, there are many examples of excellent teaching where adult art take centre stage in the lesson. Some art educators have revealed how showing children adult art can be inspirational. In this book for example, in Part 2, examples of adult art are woven into the fabric of the projects rather than left to the end. However, even if there are no hard and fast rules about when to introduce children to examples of adult culture, try to keep the qualities of originality and meaning of the children's own ideas to the fore.

Birdman boulder from Orongo, Easter Island (Rapa Nui), Polynesia

This records an annual race to celebrate the feast of the birdman. The most powerful leaders of the community each send a representative (hopu) to swim out to the nearby islet of Motu Iti. There they collect one of the first eggs laid by a sooty tern and bring it back undamaged. The winner holds the prestigious title of 'birdman' until the following year.

Thinking back to their imaginary island communities, could children create their own competition and design motifs and symbols to represent the victor, or make objects that might be awarded as a prize? The competition could also become the focus for stories, dance and music.

Rocket kite, made by Pak Timtim, from Denpasar, Bali

Groups of men from Bali fly giant kites in fierce competition. There are different categories of kite including fish kites, pinched kites that look like leaves, the sacred dragon kites, and a fantasy section in which the kite makers can let the imagination have free reign. The rocket-shaped kite won the fantasy prize at the 1998 festival. Could the children create a design for a kite for their community? Perhaps, the communities on the imaginary island come together once a year for their own kite flying festival. In Bali, a kite can also be a religious symbol of a link between heaven and earth. Could the children's kites have a symbolic meaning for their imaginary community?

Chest or forehead ornament (kapkap) from Malaita, Solomon Islands, Melanesia

Images of this kind will link well with projects about costume, fashion and body adornment. This illustration shows a kapkap, a chest or forehead ornament consisting of a disc of the white shell of a giant clam that is overlaid with an openwork disc of turtle-shell. The geometric designs vary from island to island. Sometimes the central motifs include humans, animals and birds.

Diablada dance mask from Oruro, Bolivia, 1985

The Diablada is the dance of the devils and this particular one may have been inspired by old Bolivian tales. Devils lived in the depths of mines and gave an essential but dangerous power to the inner earth. Miners would make offerings to the devil to protect them from danger and help them find the best deposits of metals like silver and tin. This is a modern example, which takes inspiration from the old traditions of the Diablada. There is a project about making masks on page 66. Children may have created their own imaginary myths and legends as part of the story strip project on page 44. The two projects could be linked together and enriched by showing children examples of masks from different parts of the world and explaining some of the meanings behind them.

Glass bottle in the form of a fish from El-Amarna, Egypt

Animals could play an important role in the imaginary communities. In this case, the fish design represents a Nile tilapia fish that hatches and shelters her young in her mouth. In ancient Egypt, this became a symbol for rebirth or regeneration. Which animals are of special significance to the children's imaginary communities? Why? How might these animals be represented in the art and design the children make?

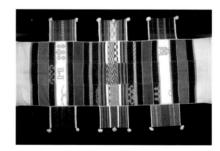

Pottery plate, from Morocco, late 20th century

This is just one of many examples from around the world that could be used to enhance a project about designs for ceramics (look back at page 55). It was made using a potting wheel. There are many types including electric, foot-propelled, and hand-turned varieties. Perhaps the children could visit a local potter's studio to see a potter's wheel in action. North African design usually is of Islamic origin. How could children use mathematical patterns as part of their designs for their imaginary community? Why would an artist prefer to use an abstract pattern rather than show a picture that can be recognised?

Cotton hammock (mboma), Mende, from Sierra Leone, Africa

This is a woven hammock, made of plain, naturally dyed cotton yarns, made on a man's tripod loom in strips of cloth, which were then sewn together. The hammock was a means of transport and used to carry important people. The weavings made by Guatemalan weavers on page 38 were used to cover food, carry children, as a shawl, and to make clothes. Could the children brainstorm all the possible uses that woven fabrics could have in their imaginary community?

African fables and stories – The King's Magic Drum

The Igbo people are from southeastern Nigeria. Oraifite is one of the towns that make up the Anaedo clan that consists of the Nnewi, Oraifite and Ichi, part of Igbo land. There is an old and powerful tradition of story telling from Oraifite. Here is a summary of a tale.

There was once a powerful king who did not like war. He owned a drum, which always provided plenty of food and drink whenever it was beaten. If anyone were tempted to declare war, the king would call his enemies together and beat the drum. There was plenty of food and drink for everyone and no fighting!

The problem was that if the owner of the drum walked over a stick or stepped over a fallen tree on the road all the food would go bad and 300 men would appear and beat the guests and the owner.

Every now and then, the king would issue an invitation to everyone to a big feast. Even wild animals such as elephants, hippopotami and leopards were invited. No one was in danger. Everyone was so pleased to be eating and drinking so well. Everyone wanted to own the drum but the king would never part with it.

One day a tortoise tricked one of the king's wives into thinking she had stolen a palm nut he owned. It was a bad thing to steal someone's food and the tortoise demanded compensation. He would only accept the drum. The king gave the tortoise the magic drum but deliberately kept quiet about the bad things that could happen to the owner.

The tortoise was delighted and took the drum home to his family saying that he was now rich as all he needed to do if they were hungry is to beat the drum. Everything went well at first and for three days he entertained many people who were so pleased to eat and drink so well. They were astonished that someone who had been so poor could now host such feasts. The tortoise became lazy and did no more work. After a few weeks, he was carrying the drum home from a neighbour's farm when he stepped over a stick.

Next morning the family were hungry so the tortoise beat the drum as usual. Only this time the house became full of men who beat the tortoise, his wife and his children badly. The tortoise was angry and was determined that everyone should suffer the same fate. So he called a feast and every one came (except the king and his wives who made excuses). Of course, as soon as the tortoise beat the drum 300 men appeared and beat all the guests. Some were hurt badly. The whole community was very angry with the tortoise. In the end, the tortoise decided to give the drum back to the king.

The king felt sorry for the tortoise and gave him a magic foo-foo tree. The tree provided enough food for each day but only if the owner visited the tree once a day. If the tree were visited more than once, the magic would be broken. The tortoise planted the tree out in the bush in a secret place. The tree provided food but one day one of the tortoise's sons decided he wanted more and tracked his father. The son bought his brothers to the tree and they eat all they could a second time around.

The next day the tree was gone. The tortoise hunted everywhere but all he could find was the prickly tie-tie palm. The tortoise told his family that they would have to eat the palm nuts and so they made their home underneath the prickly tree. Now you will always find tortoises under the prickly tie-tie palm: they have nowhere else to go for food.

This concludes Part 1 although you might like to look back at page 40. Stories from communities all over the world could enrich the kind of creative projects featured in this book. We are fortunate that in recent years, the Internet has made researching such material so much easier.

2 Identity, imagination and dreams

Where do we belong? What is our place in the social structure? What do we believe? How would we describe ourselves to others? Which cultures do we feel part of, or want to feel part of? Identity is partly about allegiance and sometimes it is an unavoidable given (we were born to be who we are). Identity is also about personality, individual characteristics and how others see us. It is, of course, the grit that gives purchase to much in art. In this section projects inspired by ideas about identity and the individual include strategies focused on imagination (animals and machines with unique identities), dreams (ways to tap into the unlimited playfulness of meaningful dreaming) and personality.

In contrast to Part 1, 'Creating cultures', the hub is the self rather than the group. But what is a self without others to see it? So as in Part 1, coming together to create, share and express ideas remains at the core of the activities. Children have the opportunity to explore ideas about individuals and in doing so understand how notions such as feelings, emotions and character can be part of what art means.

As the nineteenth century gathered pace in a quickly changing Europe, reasons for making art changed. At the beginning of the century, artists like the French painters David and Géricault made large paintings that told powerful stories. These were carefully constructed to carry complex meanings; the artist manipulated the elements of a painting (for example, light, composition, narrative, symbols, space) like a twentieth century film director. Towards the end of the century artists like Van Gogh (also working in France) were painting smaller, intensely personal visions of a world deeply coloured by their own psychology. The personality of a painting, its power to express an individual's emotions and feelings, became an important reason to make paintings and an important reason to look at paintings.

This section describes strategies that will help children discover that art can have personality, and that an individual's emotions and feelings can be part of what art means. The projects explore individuality and the self. The section also tackles the concept of abstraction taught through the filter of personality. Abstraction could be an important part of any primary school's art curriculum and the ideas described here provide ways of helping children understand how abstract art can be meaningful.

2.1
Identity

Imaginary people

If you look back to page 62 you will find a description of one way of creating imaginary people with children. The illustrations show examples of how children used templates to quickly circumvent problems that they may have had drawing figures. You can also find out more about this strategy on page 63. Figure drawing is not easy and children can quickly become discouraged. Although there are good strategies to help children draw figures from observation, our intention in this project, is to focus on imagination. Why not leave observational work on figures for another day? The imaginary human figures illustrated here are given personality and identity through the clothes they are wearing. »150

Personalities and characters

What makes up a personality? What are the qualities that characterise a unique individual? These include behaviour and temperament that, in turn, are made up of emotional and mental states. How people react in given situations often relates to their personality. Books and plays have characters but so do individuals. 'What is his character like?' This is often equivalent to asking, 'What kind of personality does he have?' There are also inner and outer characteristics. Individuals can think about themselves and make judgements about their own characters and other people can look at individuals from the outside to describe what they are like. Together with the preceding activity focused on imaginary people, this activity can enrich many other projects in this book, peopling imaginary communities with characters and personalities.

To help children create imaginary personalities, teachers could structure a set of questions in a similar way to the previous project about creating imaginary people, only this time focus on emotions and behavioural traits. One tactic could be to use the 'key idea' strategy. Look forward to page 135 for examples of how the concept of key ideas can help with planning this kind of project.

Why not start by creating an imaginary personality or character with the whole class? You could try these kinds of questions to help structure the activity. Remember that in this case we are talking about one individual.

What age is our imaginary person going to be? Are they a boy, a girl, a man or a women? (Or a monster, ghost, animal, spirit, god, super hero, etc.) What are some of the things that they like to do best? What are some of the things that they like to do least? What do they like to eat? What kinds of clothes do they like to wear? What is their hair style like? What is the expression on their face like? If you met him/her, what would you like about him/her? If you met him/her, what would you dislike about him/her? Let's give this personality a name.

There could be many sub questions about details. 'Play back' children's ideas by summarising what they have been saying. The next stage is to ask children to consider how this kind of person might behave in certain situations. This is, after all, an acid test of personality and character. The question you ask may depend on the kind of personality already under construction, but here are some suggestions. For the sake of the example let's call the character Zanty.

Someone has played a trick on Zanty and volunteered him to sing a song in front of loads of people. He can't get out of it. What does he do?

A boy moves next door. He is a bit strange and is very unpopular. What does Zanty think about the boy? They are in the same class at school. How does he behave in school? How does he behave at home?

Zanty is walking down the road and finds £100, what does he do? What would he like to do?

An amazing thing happens. Zanty finds a magic lamp and, yes, the genie gives him three wishes. What does he wish for and why?

As you can imagine there are endless possibilities. After a short while, as they begin to get the idea, you can ask children to invent the questions as well as talk about the answers!

All the above are directed towards behaviour. Another layer of questions could be directed towards feelings. Replay the above questions and the scenarios that the children have invented but this time focus on feelings. 'How do you think Zanty feels when the unpopular boy talks to him in school? How does Zanty feel when he finds the £100?'

This whole activity could also be focused on creating depth of personality for characters in stories that children may have created as they formed the imaginary cultures described in Part 1.

Looking at portraits in art

The two previous activities, creating imaginary people, personalities and characters make an excellent starting point for talking about portraits in art. Children can go on to make imaginary and real portraits of their own.

Here is one idea about how teachers could structure such a project. In this example, the teacher finds different examples of portraits in different media. For example, a representational painting of a person, a photographic portrait, a sculptural portrait, an abstracted portrait from the twentieth century and a portrait of an imaginary or mythical character, being or personality. For example, the Tate Gallery at www.tate.org.uk has an option to search its bank of on-line images by subject. To resource this activity you could look through the categories, 'emotions concepts and ideas', 'people', 'symbols and personifications' and 'work and occupations'. Each of these categories breaks down further into layers of ideas. For example, 'symbols and personifications', sub-divides into sections such as 'birth and death', 'gender' and 'mythological'. Again, this echoes the possibility of planning using 'key ideas' to help structure projects that have meaning at their centre.

If you are looking at portraits, you could also include representations of people from different cultures.

For example, the British Museum in London has an on-line database of images from world cultures at www.thebritishmuseum.ac.uk/compass.

If you are going to project these digital images it is so important to try to maximise the viewing conditions. Many classrooms are very light and weak projectors make poor quality images that show little detail and none of the powerful qualities of the original. Colour, in particular, is lost. Are you able to organise a place to show the children quality images? It may even be better to print colour copies of the portraits and hand these to the children to talk about rather than persist with a larger but washed out image on screen.

I have collected five different kinds of portrait to show you. First of all let's make a list together of everything we can see in each portrait. I have five columns, one for each portrait and we can note the various ideas down under each.

It is always very helpful if children are given a chance to share ideas about the simple and obvious items they can see in the art object. Next, try the kinds of questions you may have used in the previous activity, age, appearance, likes, dislikes and questions such as, 'If you met this character what would they be like? How would you feel?' Try inventing questions, which mirror the examples linked to behaviour. Just as

before, if children are comfortable with the idea, they could make up their own questions.

Now focus on visual qualities like colours and textures and then on practical ideas about how the object was made. What tools and materials did the artist use?

Close the activity by asking children to talk about what they like and dislike about each of the portraits. Ask them to choose which one they would like to see at home every day. Why? Which one would they least like to see? Why?

Here are some spin off ideas, linked to other projects in this book. For example, children could make a television presentation about the portraits, (see page 46). They could pretend to be the figure in the portrait and another child could interview them on camera (see page 131).

Children could use photocopies of the images and look at different ways of changing the image. Look at the projects on using a photocopier and collage later in Part 2 (see page 97). The question that might lead this idea could be, 'What could you add to the portrait or how could you change it to alter its personality and character?'.

Making portraits

Here is a summary of a project for making imaginary portraits that picks up on the teaching strategies described in the previous few pages. This imaginary portrait project is best organised in conjunction with other activities in this section and could be linked to making observational portraits, which could either follow or precede making imaginary portraits depending on your teaching style.

You are going to draw and paint an imaginary portrait. First of all we need to practise making up the different parts of your character.

You have a large sheet of paper taped onto your drawing board with masking tape. I have given everyone a fibre-tipped writing pen.

Practise inventing five different kinds of nose. Here are some ideas: pointed, long and thin, fat and bulbous, like an animals nose, hooked, huge!

Practise making five different kinds of eyes. Here are some ideas: big round and starring, narrow, with really long eye lashes, jagged, beautiful!

Practise making five different hair styles...

Children could also refer to portraits by adult artists they have already discovered and copy elements from these onto their sheets. They should have a rich collection of ideas. This can be enhanced by notes. For example, words could be used to describe colours, emotions and other thoughts linked to the drawings. Although, to keep the activity simple and free flowing, children have been asked to use one drawing media, a fibre tipped pen, they could also make these experiments in pastels, felt pens, crayons and by collage from photocopies and print outs.

 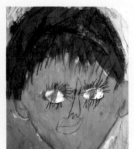

There are three approaches to drawing or painting the finished imaginary portrait. Children could attempt to illustrate a personality or character that they have already created as part of earlier work in this section; they could illustrate a character from a story that they have read or created themselves (look back at page 40, for example); or they might create a character in freestyle, as it were, simply combining various physical characteristics in a playful kind of way.

Children can build their portrait using facial components. Start with the nose, go on to eyes and mouth and then add the shape of the head, hair, ears, neck, shoulders and so on. Many additional details can be added as children work. Pimples, wrinkles, moustaches, hats, earrings, false eyelashes, tattoos, nose studs, etc! **»150**

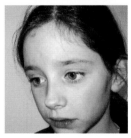

Digital portraits

Children can also transform their own appearance to exaggerate, hide or change their own personality. Digital cameras can record these changes or children can change digital photographs of themselves in many different ways. Changes to images can be made using computer software or traditional media, working onto print outs and photocopies.

This is quite a simple way of tapping into the portraiture theme. Here are some ideas that might kick-start a photographic project.

How can the hats people wear change their personality? Teachers and children could make a collection of hats and discuss how the same person could be seen differently depending on the hat they are wearing.

How do facial expressions reflect emotions and what people are feeling? Ask children to practise different facial expressions that show emotion. They can also use their hands if they think it will help. It is sometimes useful to exaggerate expressions for the

camera. Anger, shyness, joy, despair, longing, frustration, fear, terror, confidence and many other ideas could all come into play. Children could work in pairs, one taking the photograph, the second posing. They then swap jobs. Look forward to page 138 for some suggestions about using a camera. In this case, a tripod is probably not necessary but ask children to think about how close or far away they would like to be to the subject. What looks the best, the subject and their emotional expression filling the frame or a little distant from it?

Look back at page 65 and the projects about costume. Making costumes and accessories could be led by ideas in this section about character and personality, rather than by imaginary islands and communities. Alternatively, you could try this project after the children have created imaginary communities. In this case, the digital portraits will be linked to the personalities that inhabit the communities or the stories that were generated (look back at page 42). Face painting adds yet another dimension.

For the simplest and clearest results, it is probably better to have a plain, neutral background against which children can photograph the head and shoulders of the model. However, backgrounds and sets could become a feature of the project. One easy to manage variation is to offer children a choice of plain coloured fabrics that could be hung behind the model.

Teachers could go on to suggest that children manipulate their portraits using computer software. There are often filters and effects that can instantly change or distort the character of the shot. Words can be added, other visual motifs could be cut and pasted on to the image. Children could use simple paint and draw tools to colour and adapt their image even further. All the digital images can be used as starting points either for new work or as a base onto which children draw, collage, print or paint using traditional media. However, children could simply aim for a photographic end product, using the digital camera. The photographs can be printed, displayed and valued as art.

The reader may be wondering why this section about abstraction immediately follows ideas about identity. First, abstraction provides a useful contrast with the highly figurative character of the work described in the first pages of Part 2. The differences and interrelationships between figuration and abstraction dominated twentieth century art and design. Teachers can help children understand that they can use both realistic and abstract ideas as they work, particularly in design. Just look around your own home. The kinds of design you find on ceramics, fabrics and flooring will be abstract, although in many cases the abstraction could be traced back to the observed world, especially if we were able to interview the designer and ask about his or her inspiration!

Second, starting with qualities such as feelings, emotions and human character is a featured approach to teaching abstraction in this book. This naturally complements ideas about identity, personality and character. For example, paintings can be said to have personalities and we can help children talk about painting using the same kind of vocabulary. Or, to put this another way, that we can help children talk about art by using the same kinds of words and concepts that we use to talk about an individual's personality, character, emotions and feelings. Last, teaching abstraction in the primary school classroom offers the opportunity to introduce two key ideas that will help children understand more about the arts – notions of form and notions of content. In visual art, form could be said to encompass concepts such as colour, space, shape, materials and processes, whereas a

2.2
Abstraction

discussion of content might include meaning and significance. Form and content come together in art as objects that have aesthetic and expressive power. Adults and children can enjoy both the physical and cerebral aspects of art.

Working abstractly has a number of other benefits. Abstraction also can be a vehicle for teaching art for art's sake. That is, the aesthetic, non-literal qualities of the experience of art can come to the fore. The sheer experience of materials and visual qualities is enjoyed for its own sake without the need to overlay self-conscious meanings. Removed from the pressure to produce realistic images, children who have difficulties with observational drawing can find success. Children are all, more or less, placed on the same footing as they work and sometimes the apparently less able or more individual children who

would not usually come to the fore find themselves leading the way. The endless possibilities of abstraction, the often playful energy, promotes risk taking and the acceptance of the unexpected, two helpful characteristics of creativity. Children also experience and learn something about one of the great themes of twentieth century art and design, since the impact of abstract design is visible in every home, car, office and public building in countless fabrics, wall coverings, decorative schemes, domestic objects and architectural details. »150

Making abstract drawings

This project will work best if you can find a large space to work in such as the school hall, and if you can use large sheets (or better still large rolls) of paper. But all this work is still worthwhile even if children are limited to A2 sheets.

Focus the children on words that could be used to describe a person's character. For example, you and the children might have recorded words like timid, shy, quiet, organised, loud, a show off, fussy, precise, eccentric and colourful as part of work on identity in the previous section.

Let's take one example. Ask the children to stand up and find a small space to move around in. Ask them to pretend that they are a timid person who is shy and quiet and afraid of lots of different things.

If you were shy and timid how would you stand? Would you stand tall and straight and open your arms wide to welcome every one? Or, would you tend to curl yourself up a little to become smaller and less noticeable and hide your head and not look at anyone?

Ask the children to practise being shy and timid. Then contrast this with eccentric and loud.

If you were a loud person and a bit eccentric how might you stand? Would you be quiet and hidden away or would you stand out as tall and as noticeable as possible? Would you be completely ordinary looking or would an eccentric person have something odd about the way they stand?

The contrasts help children to understand the idea that they can become different kinds of personality and take on characteristics, acting out simple actions, movements or poses to illustrate differences. There is exaggeration here which is inevitable and useful. If, during the earlier project, you had talked about emotions and feelings, words such as exuberant, carefree, lonely, sad and confused could come into play. But as you can see, there is a very indistinct boundary between emotion, characteristics and personality in this project.

The children are now going to make abstract lines and marks that link with some of the words and concepts we have been exploring. Give the children a large piece of paper and two distinct drawing implements such as piece of charcoal and a marker pen. If you have a large roll of paper spread this out across the floor and you can give each child in the group a section of their own to work in. If the paper is very large the children could sit in the middle of their section when they start and you could suggest that their drawings could surround them and that they only fill the empty space where their bodies have been. But let's suppose the children have A2 paper. This could be inexpensive paper as each child may use three or four sheets. If you have drawing boards these provide flexible and mobile work spaces so that the children can work on the floor or sit with the board on their knees a little away from a table, resting the top of the board against the side of the table creating an angle. However, in this particular project, having the paper on the floor allows children to move around more freely and perhaps they can escape from the idea of there being a fixed top and a bottom of their drawing. To illustrate what can happen let's take two contrasting characteristics or personalities, exuberant and shy

Imagine that you are an exuberant person. Exuberant people are likely to be lively, energetic, high-spirited, cheerful and enthusiastic. Imagine you are an exuberant person and you are going to meet a really good friend who you have not seen for a long time. They are standing over there by the wall. What would you do? How would you approach them, slowly and carefully or quickly and energetically? What would you do with your arms? When you get close to them how would you shake their hand? Practise greeting someone in the character of an exuberant person.

Now imagine you are really shy. Shy people are likely to be timid, quiet, withdrawn, bashful and embarrassed. Imagine you are a shy person and you are going to meet someone who you have never seen before. They are standing over there by the wall. What would you do? How would you approach them; slowly and carefully or quickly and energetically? What would you do with your arms? What would you do with your head? How would you walk? What would your body posture be like? When you get close how would you shake their hand? Practise greeting someone but in the character of a shy person.

The idea here is that children can see clearly that there are differences between how the two different personalities move and act in a very similar situation. This can now be translated into abstract drawing. You could ask them:

How would an exuberant person cover the paper in lines and marks? They might be excited, energetic and enthusiastic. Can you think of different ways of making marks in an excited way, an energetic way and in an enthusiastic way?

Give the children the drawing materials and suggest that they move around the paper acting out how an exuberant person might cover the paper in lines and marks. You may need to stop them working quite soon after they start; they will work very quickly and it is better to be able to see the marks and lines clearly. If the children work for too long the paper will simply become covered in an indecipherable mass. Now you can change the paper only this time you suggest:

How would a shy person cover the paper in lines and marks? They might be timid, embarrassed and hesitant. Can you think of different ways of making marks in a timid way, an embarrassed way and in a hesitant way.

Again, the children could move around the paper acting out how a shy person might draw on the paper. It might be worth reminding them that perhaps a shy person would not cover the paper completely at all. They would just be too embarrassed to make such a big drawing!

This exercise can be repeated using the rich vocabulary we use to talk about character and personality, with the emphasis on the children taking on and acting out the different personality traits as they are drawing. They may produce a great deal of work quickly. If you are in a large space such as the hall, there may well be enough room to spread out the drawings on the floor so that the children can see what they have done and talk about the differences. If you are in the classroom try using one small strip of masking tape on the top of the paper to temporarily tape the drawings on the wall. This will cover any existing display but the masking tape will not damage anything if it is lightly applied and gently removed. The drawings will be higgledy-piggledy but the children will be able to see their work right away.

Looking back at the project we have just described, you might encourage the children to talk about exuberant marks, timid lines, hesitant marks and energetic lines. Can they describe the differences between the various abstract drawings?

The final practical session is to invite the children to create their own abstract drawings that build on what they know about different ways of making lines and marks that relate to character and personality. They could, for example, choose two or three different personalities and try to organise their paper to include each of them. This will involve some kind of division or structure in the drawing. To help them you could suggest that they can draw shapes as well as lines and marks. Another idea could be to cover the paper in lines and marks relating to one kind of personality and then go over the top with marks and lines that express something of a contrasting character. A third idea is to allow the children to invent a personality of their own that has several characteristics according to how they feel at any one time. For example, brave but exhausted or desolate but secure. Can they make an abstract drawing that reflects their ideas in some way?

The concept of repetition and pattern may be useful and help less able children find a structure for this more complex and difficult work. Colour adds a whole new dimension to the project, as does the addition of formal elements. For example, another teaching strategy could focus on concepts such as space, shape and line. This removes the emphasis on describing marks in terms of personality and character. Instead, purely visual ideas are at the core of the work. This begins to fill the art for art's sake model of abstract art hinted at in the introduction to this section. That is, abstract art which is more about aesthetic form rather than expressive content. For example, children could think about space in terms of overlapping (if one motif partially overlaps another it can appear in front) and in terms of scale (how a very small motif placed near to a large motif can make the small element seem further away). Invite children to explore how it is possible to use ideas about scale to create quite dramatic abstract effects! In a tantalising twist that neatly illustrates the form versus content dilemma, this spatial drama can be described in expressive rather than formal terms. For example, a vast, overwhelming shape dominates the drawing, dwarfing a timid, powerless shape which, is receding quickly into the far distance.

The question of teacher control versus child choice is again an issue to consider. If you give the children freedom to work in their own way, without excessive direction, you may find that some children begin to add recognisable motifs, rather than continuing with purely abstract drawing. These semi-abstract drawings can be fascinating, except that, as the teacher, you had in mind an abstract end product. This kind of dilemma is ever present when teaching art. There are no obvious answers except that each project will throw up new experiences, each teacher has their own style of teaching and each child will respond in a different way. In the end it is all a matter of judgement.

Looking at abstract paintings

Paris
Maria Helena Vieira da Silva
Oil on canvas, 1952

Find a number of reproductions of abstract paintings. Or better still, visit an art gallery that is exhibiting abstract art. It will always make a difference if children can see the work in real life. Although working from reproductions is perfectly feasible, consider the quality of the image the children will see. For example, is the image too small for children to really see detail, especially if you are showing it to the whole class? If you are projecting an image, is the picture the children see washed out because the room is too light? Can they see the quality of colour, for example. The better the reproduction and the conditions in which children can see it, the better will be their response to it.

We are going to help children talk about abstract art using a descriptive vocabulary that they will discover themselves as the teacher uses structured layers of questions. It is important to show children paintings that are really different to each other. Try to find three examples that have large variations in qualities such as colour, surface, size, marks, character and energy. We have chosen three painters from the Tate Gallery's collection and their work is illustrated here. The first is Bert Irvin whose huge paintings of sweeping, broad and highly coloured marks evoke a tremendous energy. The second artist is Maria Helena Vieira Da Silva whose painting, Paris, is delicately coloured, intricate and geometric and painted with such a soft touch that it makes a perfect counter point to Irvin's bold exuberant energy. The final artist is Bernard Cohen whose complicated layers of complex abstract marks, lines and colours provide a further contrast. Teachers can find images of all the paintings mentioned in this mini project in the searchable database at www.tate.org.uk.

First ask the children the most simple question of all, 'What can you see?' Ask the question of each of the three paintings. Try to keep a note of what they say or if they are working in groups ask a secretary from each group to note down the responses. It is very effective if you can 'play back' the children's responses as it helps to highlight what they have said. Also any new vocabulary used by individual children can be kept for later use. Children will reference real world ideas to help describe what they can see. 'It looks like a...' will be a phrase repeated again and again. These ideas can be very informative. Children's comments will also be very different if they have already made abstract drawings as suggested by the previous project.

Next, ask the children to talk about some of the qualities of the paintings. For example, how would they describe the colours they can see? Are the colours, bright, dull, glaring, harmonious, delicate, soft, crazy, pale or subtle? If you are focusing on colours try to home in on the qualities of a particular colour like green. What does the green remind you of? Moss? Grass? Bottles? Spring leaves? Seaweed? Apart from colours, other qualities that you could focus on include shapes, lines and marks and the surface of the painting (its texture). If you would like the children to think about the space in an abstract painting try asking them to point out the place in the painting which looks the closest to them and then ask them to find the place which looks the furthest away. If they were travelling into the painting from the front to the back, what colours (or other qualities such as shapes, lines and marks etc.) would they pass on the way.

The third layer of questions is about character and personality. Ask the children to think about the artist:

What kind of person would have made a painting like this? If you met the artist, what do you think they would be like? What kinds of things do you think the artist likes to do? What would the artist wear? What would their hair be like? Describe their personality. If you could visit their studio, where they work, what would it be like? For example, would it be very tidy or in a complete mess? What kinds of objects do they think the artist would enjoy? What kind of music would they listen to?

The aim of these questions is to begin to introduce children to a language for describing abstract paintings that is equivalent to the language that we use to describe people. As the discussions come to an end, remind the children of what they have said and suggest that they could use the same kinds of words to describe the painting itself. Perhaps they described the artist Bert Irvin as being energetic, crazy, daring and bold. Whereas Maria Vieira da Silva is quieter, gentler and detailed. You can see how such vocabulary can have a value in unlocking the 'personality' of a painting.

Right:
Matter of Identity
Bernard Cohen
Oil, tempera and metallic
paint on canvass, 1963

Below:
St Germain
Bert Irvin
Acrylic on Canvass, 1995

Emotion, feeling, character and personality are part of the make up of paintings and how they affect us. Another way of thinking about this is to note just how helpful it can be for an adult to understand something of the biography of an artist or a musician as part of the process of understanding more about their work. One note of caution, this is an exercise to help children see how to describe abstract paintings using a similar vocabulary used to describe a person's character or personality. It does not imply that the we can say for sure that Bert Irvin, for example, is energetic, crazy, daring and bold!

During the discussions children will have formed their own opinions about the paintings you have shown them. Now is a good time to ask them to comment on what they like and dislike about the paintings and how the paintings make them feel. You could ask them to talk about something that they like and dislike about each of the three paintings, say, making six comments in all. Ask them if they would like to have the paintings (or the reproductions) on a wall in their house or even in their bedroom. The children will be talking about how, as well as whether or not, they value each of the paintings.

Large abstract paintings

There are many different techniques teachers can use to teach children painting. When the National Curriculum for Art was introduced in England, Wales and Northern Ireland in the 1990s, children were often encouraged to learn how to mix colours. This often meant that children used very small quantities of colour. Some teachers showed them a dash and dab technique that echoed French Impressionism. However, for this project children are going to need large quantities of colour. It is best if these are mixed in advance and stored in plastic vessels of some kind such as large yoghurt pots or small ice cream containers. Containers with lids will help keep the paint fresh. To help make the project more practical ask each group of five or six children to mix ten or twelve colours between them. In effect each child will mix two tubs of colour. Show them how they can squeeze the ready mix colour into the container and then add a second and possibly a third colour to create a range of colours for the group to use. They should not only think about a range of hue (different kinds of colours) but also of tone (light and dark colours). Plastic spoons are good to stir the paint and the children could add a little (but not too much) water to help mix the paint well. The consistency of thick pouring cream is good to aim for. Tell the children not to fill the paint containers too full, half full is about right. »150

To help give structure to the mixing activity you could set a number of challenges. For example, could a child make two contrasting colours? Or, they could each make one shade of a primary colour (for example a red with a hint of green to create a slightly darker, deeper red than the one from the ready mix tube) and one shade of a secondary colour (for example yellow and blue to make green with a hint of white to make it paler)? It is a good idea to discuss the various possibilities in advance. You might organise a mini-demonstration workshop with the children before they mix their own colours. Liquid acrylic colours are more expensive but the increase in pigment quality is significant. If the school can afford the additional cost you will be rewarded by paintings with richer and subtler colour.

When the group has mixed a good range of colours ask each child to make a colour sample chart by painting a stripe or block of each colour onto some paper. This can be a good opportunity to remind them about how discipline can be helpful. For example, we are going to ask the children to always wash their brush or painting implement before putting it into new colour. The main reason for this is that they are going to be sharing the colours and it only takes one dirty brush full of a red to completely ruin the green pot! But even if the children are working individually with their own set of colours, they will see the importance of keeping the pots of colour clean.

Assuming children have had the chance to both look at abstract paintings and make abstract drawings connected to personalities, they should have plenty of ideas about the enormous variety of marks, lines, shapes and colours they can use. The paintings of Bernard Cohen illustrated on page 89 are clearly built up in layers and this is a strategy the you and the children can keep in mind.

The very best support for large paintings is stretched canvas. It is both light in weight and strong. It is now possible to buy ready stretched and primed canvas very cheaply. Look out for discounted canvas in craft and modelling suppliers, discount book and hobby stores and even in specialist artists' merchants. These come in a range of sizes, buy the largest size that is both practical and affordable. You will need one large canvas for each group of children, or perhaps, smaller canvases for individual children to use.

Before the children begin painting ask each child to prepare five different abstract motifs. If you like, five bits or parts of an abstract painting that they think they could be used in the collaborative piece. Each abstraction could have its own unique character or personality made up of a special combination of shapes, colours, marks and lines. Emphasise this with children. You are looking for contrasts and differences. Some children will instinctively revert to drawing recognisable motifs. It is a matter of judgement as to whether you want to stop this and insist they return to pure abstraction or let it continue and see the effect that recognisable motifs will have in the final painting.

Is the painting going to be made up of layers? If it is, teachers will need to set at least three painting sessions. The first session is to cover the canvas in a ground of colour. These 'backgrounds' could be monochromatic, atmospheric or geometric. They could be soft and pale, strong and powerful or dark. Each background could have a mixture of all these ideas. Brainstorm the possibilities before the group starts to paint. Children could take it in turns to complete the background.

For the second session children can begin to add their abstract motifs on top of the first layer. Find a strategy to help them. For example, they could start in the middle of the canvas and take it in turns adding their motifs until they reach the outer edges. They could divide the canvas into bands or areas and each fill one of these. They could adopt a random strategy and take it in turns adding the motifs wherever they choose until the whole canvas is full.

The third session gives children a chance to add detail, paint out areas they dislike and discuss ideas about anything that they could do to help unify the finished work. Oil pastels can be useful here, as they offer children the possibility of adding a variety of strongly pigmented colour on top of the painted areas. These can help define and delineate them, or, in other words, resolve them.

The children will also need to be disciplined in the way they handle the paint. Ask them to keep all the colour pots on a protected work surface. There should be a large, half full, container of water and ample sponges and rags to dry brushes. If they have mixed a good range of colours in advance, they may not need mixing palettes. However, if you would like children to be able to mix smaller quantities of colour, why not use paper plates as mixing palettes? These can be thrown away when all the paint is used up or the colours become too polluted. If the children are using a colour from a pot or from the paper plate, ask them to take the colour with them to the painting, hold the pot or palette in one hand and a brush in the other. They will need a choice of different sizes and styles of paint brush. The canvas should be a little away from the paint area and flat on a table so that children can walk around each of the four sides and work from which ever direction they choose. Protect the floor under and just around the table. Insist that when children are painting they do not walk outside a dedicated dirty area. If you are using acrylic paints, children should wear old clothes as well as aprons or old shirts.

If the canvases are on easels, make sure that the paint is not too liquid. It should not run down the canvas. If it does children will not be able to control the results. Having said this, there are quite a few contemporary painters who have used the idea of liquid, running paint. The bottom line is that in reality there are no special rules, only the ones that the teacher and children use to bring thought and control to the work. Decide on the these 'rules' with the children in advance. Far from inhibiting creativity, a clear framework that helps give discipline to the activity, will support children and give them confidence to work creatively inside this secure precinct of ideas.

We have been describing group paintings. Clearly, children could work as individuals using similar structures and techniques. Throughout this book, the view is that children's work is enriched when they can create and share meaning. Talking about all aspects of making abstract art, both before, during and after the project will help this process. Why not see how individual children, particularly those who show a keen interest, respond to the challenge of making their own, personal and individual abstract painting following this project. Don't forget about the stimulus provided by looking at abstract paintings. A data bank of images of abstract art can be found at www.tate.org.uk.

The sections that follow look in more detail at different ways a teacher can use external stimuli to spark a project into life in which children can find the freedom to be imaginative. There is a constant tension between ideas led by the teacher (for example, by controlling the specific stimuli children experience, or by controlling a structure through which children work towards their outcomes) and between the potential for children to organise themselves, find their own stimuli and decide on the way they can go on to express imaginative ideas. Children who find it difficult to use their imagination freely will appreciate more teacher support, in the form of suggestions and starting points. Equally, children who may be very imaginative may find working independently within a structure difficult and in turn, appreciate a teacher's support. However, with the compromises and practical realities that teaching the arts inevitably entails, it is possible to keep to the principle articulated in this book – that it is better when meaning is created by children. In the examples that follow. Meaning comes partly in response to what they read, see or hear. From these kinds of starting points, imagination can be given a free rein.

2.3
All about dreams

Talking about dreams

How would you like to start the project? Do you start by encouraging children to talk and think about their existing ideas and experiences of dreams? Do you start with a stimulus? Could you start by teaching children a skill that they will be able to use later in the project?

Here are some possible questions for children together with possible answers:

What is a dream?

You have dreams when you are asleep, Something you want a lot, an ambition, something not real.

What is a dream like?

Dreams are weird, Not real, scary, like wanting something a lot.

Are there different kinds of dreams?

Nightmares, happy dreams, day dreams.

What happens in dreams?

Strange things, you can fly, you don't know if its real.

Do you remember your dreams?

Who would like to talk about a dream they have had? Who would like to describe their dream?

Are there any differences between a dream world and a real world?

How could children interpret dreams? For example, the appearance of an airplane in a dream could mean exciting times ahead. It could also mean coming success. If crossroads appear in a dream this could mean that the dreamer to needs to make a decision.

Let's make a list of objects that you might see, find or use in a dream. We could try to make up an interpretation for each of them.

Talking about dreams in this way does not need any external stimulus. As an alternative, start by looking at dream art from different cultures, an extract from film, a poem or fictional story, a real life story told by an adult.

Why not start by reading the children fiction or poetry? For example, the childrens storybook *Where the Wild Things Are* has a particular poetry, use of language, and strange ideas that are very appropriate to dreams. You could try popular children's fiction, extracts from Harry Potter, for example. Why not look for extracts from classical children's literature as in this example from *Alice in Wonderland* (Lewis Carroll, 1872).

'Come and look at him!' the brothers cried, and they each took one of Alice's hands, and led her up to where the King was sleeping.
'Isn't he a lovely sight?' said Tweedledum.
Alice couldn't say honestly that he was. He had a tall red night-cap on, with a tassel, and he was lying crumpled up into a sort of untidy heap, and snoring loud – 'fit to snore his head off!' as Tweedledum remarked.

'I'm afraid he'll catch cold with lying on the damp grass,' said Alice, who was a very thoughtful little girl. 'He's dreaming now,' said Tweedledee: 'and what do you think he's dreaming about?' Alice said 'Nobody can guess that.'

'Why, about you!' Tweedledee exclaimed, clapping his hands triumphantly. 'And if he left off dreaming about you, where do you suppose you'd be?'

'Where I am now, of course,' said Alice.
'Not you!' Tweedledee retorted contemptuously. 'You'd be nowhere. Why, you're only a sort of thing in his dream!'

'If that there King was to wake,' added Tweedledum, 'you'd go out – bang! – just like a candle!'

'I shouldn't!' Alice exclaimed indignantly. 'Besides, if I'm only a sort of thing in his dream, what are you, I should like to know?' 'Ditto,' said Tweedledum. 'Ditto, ditto!' cried Tweedledee.
He shouted this so loud that Alice couldn't help saying 'Hush! You'll be waking him, I'm afraid, if you make so much noise.'

'Well, it's no use your talking about waking him,' said Tweedledum, 'when you're only one of the things in his dream. You know very well you're not real'. 'I am real!' said Alice, and began to cry.'

Why not start from a factual event or report? Find texts about sleepwalking, premonitions, and real life dreams. A different project narrative would be prompted by asking children to respond to Martin Luther King's famous speech:

'I have a dream that one day on the red hills of Georgia the sons of former slaves and the sons of former slave owners will be able to sit down together at a table of brotherhood. I have a dream that one day even the state of Mississippi, a desert state, sweltering with the heat of injustice and oppression, will be transformed into an oasis of freedom and justice. I have a dream that my four children will one day live in a nation where they will not be judged by the colour of their skin but by the content of their character. I have a dream today. I have a dream that one day the state of Alabama, whose governor's lips are presently dripping with the words of interposition and nullification, will be transformed into a situation where little black boys and black girls will be able to join hands with little white boys and white girls and walk together as sisters and brothers. I have a dream today.'

You could ask: *What is your dream for a better world? What do you dream of?*

This kind of dream, a dream for a better or ideal world or dreams about attaining success and being a better person will link into other projects in this book. An island community could have a dream. Look back at page 31. Discussion of tenets of belief could lead to thoughts about dreaming (even praying) for good qualities in imaginary lives (see page 116). Individuals, including imaginary people, could have these kinds of dreams.

Dreamings

Teachers could start this project by sharing a story from the 'Dreaming' of indigenous Australians – one of the oldest continuing cultures on earth. Despite the cataclysmic disruption of the ancient and harmonious way of living and thinking when Caucasians invaded their homelands, indigenous Australians still use their idea of dreaming to express spiritual beliefs. However, Howard Morphy[1] warns in his book *Aboriginal Art* that 'the words Dreaming and Dreamtime should not be understood in their ordinary English sense, but as words that refer to a unique and complex religious concept. The Dreaming exists independently of the linear time of everyday life and the temporal sequence of historical events ... [but what] was there in the beginning, underlies the present and is a determinant of the future ... The Dreamtime is as concerned with space as with time – it refers to origins and powers that are located in places and things.'

In other traditional cultures, stories of the magical and spiritual that help explain the physical and mental world of people, can be expressed as myths. Today, there is a rich seam of mythological stories from all over the world on the Internet. These old ideas infuse, refract and fracture, are reformed and dissipated by countless retellings in countless contexts for countless reasons. There is a sadness here (smaller, weaker cultures are assimilated, even plundered) but there is also the opportunity of showing children how they can create their own stories that make sense of ideas, feeling and the hugely complex world around them.

Why not start by sharing an ancient story from one of the world's many cultures? These may not be dreams, but for us they are imaginings and to children they will be dream like. Here is an example from Australia that is retold in a simplified form. The text is adapted from Donni Hakanson's book 'Oracle of the Dreamtime'.[2] Teachers can find further accounts of indigenous Australian dreaming in publications and on the Internet. Look back at page 40 and the ideas about creating stories and story strips. Could children, inspired by magical mythology, create their own imaginings that explain something about the physical world or human behaviour?

The Rainbow Serpent was sleeping far underground in the centre of the earth. After a long time she woke up. She crawled all the way through the dirt and broke through the surface in a shower of ochre dust. Rainbow Serpent had a powerful magic and as she travelled across the flat land she made it rain heavily. Her serpent tracks filled up with water and made rivers and lakes. As she slithered over the land, milk from her breasts soaked into the ground. This made the earth fertile and forests grew. She made mountain ranges and valleys.

Rainbow Serpent woke up all the animals and birds who could live on the earth. Creatures that live in water were woken too. Fish, frogs, eels and turtles. She bought a man and a women from the womb of the earth. She taught man and women how to live in peace and harmony with all the animals and how to live together and share with one another. She showed man and women how to pass on their knowledge to children.

Man and woman were the caretakers of the land. Rainbow Serpent had finished her task. But she stayed and went to live in a water hole where she looks after the water creatures. If anyone is greedy and takes more fish than they need, Rainbow Serpent will come out to punish whoever breaks the tribal law. »**150**

[1] Morphy, H (1998) 'Aboriginal Art', London, Phaidon Press.

[2] Donni Hakanson (1998) 'Oracle of the Dreamtime', Llandeilo, Cygnus Books.

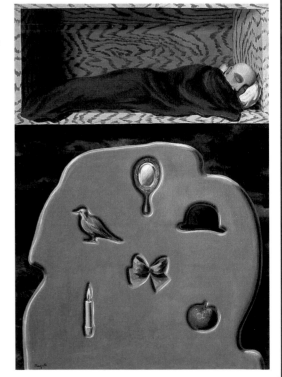

Left
Landscape from a Dream
Paul Nash, 1936-38

Right
The Reckless Sleeper
René Magritte, 1928

Dreams in art

Apart from mythologies, literature and factual accounts, much Western art has been inspired by dreams. Why not show children images by artists like Chagall, Dali or Magritte? Indeed, most of the Surrealists! For example, talk about Magritte's painting, 'The Reckless Sleeper, or 'Landscape from a Dream' by British artist, Paul Nash. Both paintings, illustrated opposite, are from Tate's collection. In a commentary on 'The Reckless Sleeper' it is stated:

'A figure sleeps in a wooden alcove or box above a dark cloudy sky. The way into this space is barred by a tablet embedded with everyday objects, which are displayed as in a book for children. As Magritte knew, some or all of them could also be read as Freudian symbols. This combination of different possible interpretations adds to the painting's suggestion of dream-like unease and disorientation.'

In a further comment on 'Landscape from a Dream' it is remarked:

'This is one of Nash's finest, and most surreal paintings. Its subject is typical of the Surrealists' fascination with Sigmund Freud's theories of the power of dreams to reveal the unconscious. Nash has chosen various elements of the scene for symbolic reasons: the self-regarding hawk belongs to the material world, while the spheres reflected in the mirror symbolize the soul.

Any artist who uses imagery in dream-like ways would be useful here, browse images on an image database and select a few to show the children. For example, in the Tate's on line collection search using the word 'dream' at www.tate.org.uk. You can use a search engine to find out more about the artist. Here is an example of how teachers could use an idea from contemporary British art as a direct stimulus to inspire a mini project narrative on the dream theme.

To establish a context, search for 'sleeping portraits' on the National Portrait Gallery, London, web site at www.npg.org.uk. Select a number of images and display or print them for children to discuss. Give each group of children one of the images. Ask them to work together to prepare some questions they could ask about the central character in the portrait and about what they might be dreaming. Ask a secretary in each group to record the questions on paper or the computer and swap the questions and the images between groups. Prepare some questions yourself and compare the children's questions with your own. Use these questions to prompt a discussion of the images. Look forward to page 135 for examples of planning strategies that are linked to using 'key ideas'. In this case, the key idea could be 'sleep is the doorway to dreams'.

Talk about the effect of a close-up portrait, you might illustrate this in practical ways using a digital camera and asking children to take portraits of each other at different distances until you are right up close to a child's face, perhaps using a macro setting to photograph just one closed eye! If a zoom is available, children could experiment with this as well.

Sam Taylor Wood filmed David Beckham asleep for a video portrait at the National Portrait Gallery. The children are unlikely to be able see the video themselves but they will be able to imagine what it is like. The video camera seems near to his face and there is a feeling of being very close to him, what was he dreaming about? What are the children dreaming about in their own digital sleep portraits?

Thinking about Sam Taylor Wood's technique, ask the children to make close-up video extracts of each other pretending to be asleep for, say, one minute. Each camera operator could prepare a commentary about what the sleeping child is dreaming. This is spoken during the minute of filming.

Before making the video ask the children to choose if they would like to hold the camera or use a tripod, discuss options with them and show the differences between hand-held and tripod mounted.

- Teach the children about the controls on the video camera.
- Allow the children to practise using the camera.
- Each child should prepare and practise the sleeping position they will use as a model.

- Each child as camera operator should practise the angle of the shot, whether the camera going to be still or moving and the closeness to the sleeping model.
- Are the children able to use light in some way? For example, could the sleeping child be in a dark cupboard or shady recess with their face illuminated by a lamp or torch? Could the children use the effects of sunlight (slatted light through half closed Venetian blinds or mottled light under some trees outside)? Could the children deliberately use shadows or reflections in some way? Advice about teaching children some skills appropriate to digital video are found on page 46.
- Children need to prepare what they going to say about the dream. Pages 46 and 47 have relevant ideas. They should time their words to last the same length of time as the video takes. They can speak into a microphone attached to the camera. This saves the need to edit or add the sound track to the images afterwards. Organise a 'screening' and talk about the results.

So far in this section, we have looked at ways of kick-starting ideas by referring to literature, cultural mythologies and western art. Why not watch an extract from a DVD? For example, you could use the first few minutes from the Harry Potter film, 'Prisoner of Azkaban'. The sequence includes the ballooning aunt and the mad journey of the night bus through the city. In the Harry Potter novel, this is created by magic but ask the children to see it as though it is a dream. Invent and use a mini-structure to help get the most out of talking about the DVD fragment. For example, use a simple series of questions to help structure the children's responses. Each section can be further sub-divided depending on how deeply you would like the children to analyse the film. For example, ask:

What did you see?
What did you feel?
What was good about what you saw?
Can you say how the film director and camera operators made us feel, excited, scared, thrilled...?

The Internet also offers a deep mine of ideas associated with dreams. Before you plan the project why not search for 'dream stories', 'dream imagery', 'dreams', 'dream narratives', 'children's dreams', for example? Spark your own and children's ideas with something unexpected! **»150**

There are five projects in this section about making dream art: using the photocopier, making up a dream using words, creating dream paintings, creating a dream-like dance and creating dream collages. The first project proposes that teachers could begin a project by teaching children a skill. This is not an approach that is used much in this publication. Rather the emphasis is on creating meaning, which drives the content of the art children make. It is in this context that skills can be taught. In other words teaching skills follows on from creating meaning. Children learn skills so that they are able to express ideas in different ways. Skills are not taught as an end in themselves. The criticism levelled against linking art with meaning in such a deliberate way is that the results can be too literal. Somehow, the sheer aesthetic excitement of working with colour, the flow of paint or the unexpected accident is missed. So, some art educationalists argue that meaning can be generated from working with the materials and processes themselves, without the need to express literal ideas; this opens children's sensibilities, and that this in itself is meaningful. This echoes a way of making art that drove much modernist art in the twentieth century. Putting arguments like these aside for a more academic discussion, it is clearly a practical possibility to begin a project by teaching children a specific skill. The potential children discover in a process could suggest ways of expressing ideas that could not have been thought of without experiencing the process first.

2.4
Making dreamy art

Using the photocopier

Children will find it useful if they are able to use a photocopier and understand some of its most important functions. An adult who is available to help children with the copier will enhance this project, especially at the start. The actual possibilities will depend on the make and model of the copier you have available. However, here is a brief example of how you might talk about the copier to children. This could be thought of as a demonstration.

Look at what this copier can do. First, here is where to put the image you want to copy. See what happens if we change the position of the image and try copying it in different positions on the glass plate. You should always keep the lid of the copier down when you are copying.

You can decide the number of copies you want to make by using this control. Do not print more than you need because each copy costs several pence.

You can change the size of the paper you are using for the copy. It can be A4 or A3.

You can use this control to enlarge or reduce the size of the copied image. Lets try a few different settings to see what happens.

You can also change the lightness or darkness of the image. Let's practise by testing your images on darker or lighter settings.

You can copy a copy of an image or even a copy of a copy of a copy of an image changing the settings each time. You could change the position of the image on the glass bed as well.

You could experiment by cutting up your image and putting the parts together in a different way before you make the copy.

You could try adding other images in your copy. Experiment by placing them between the paper with the image you want to copy and the glass of the copier.

Another possibility is to cut shapes out of paper and use these to mask your image by placing them between the paper with the image you want to copy and the glass of the copier. You can even cut holes in the shapes that are the masks!

What other objects could we put onto the glass bed of the copier? I wonder how a collection of objects like leaves, rubber bands, string, paper clips etc., would look? Don't forget that we can change the lightness and darkness of the image and change its size.

After the demonstration give the children a number of specific tasks so that they can practise using the copier and its functions. This lesson would be helpful if you are going on to the collage project at the end of the chapter.

You may decide to simply use this one technique to create images in response to the dream theme. Children can hand colour and add to their images with other media such as felt, pens, pastels and paint.

The photocopier can also be used to transfer children's images to acetate, a transparent plastic film. These acetates can in turn be projected using an overhead projector on to large sheets of paper or card. Children can use the projected image as a template to enlarge their work.

Making up a dream story

Here is an example of a project about creating a dream story using props and the children's own words. This project is designed for a group of around six children, although a whole class should be able to work in groups at the same time.

Bring in a random selection of simple objects. For example, a candle, an alarm clock, a mobile phone, a glass of water, chocolate, a toy car. Alternatively, ask the children to choose and bring into school something of their own from home. (This is likely to be a toy, a photograph, a book, an item of clothing, a game, a piece of sports equipment or a simple household object).

Each child in the group chooses and holds one of the objects. Let's suppose we start with the child holding the alarm clock. The teacher could begin by asking:

Your clock does strange and unusual things. Your clock could help you do strange and unusual things, can you tell us about your strange and unusual clock?

Move on to the child with the mobile phone and ask:

Your mobile phone does strange and unusual things, or could help you do strange and unusual things, can you tell us about your strange and unusual mobile phone?

When every one in the group has had a turn, ask the children to create three characters who are going to appear in the dream. You could open this up for general discussion and act as a chairperson. Alternatively, you could give the children some guide

ideas to help focus their choice. For example, one character could be an animal, another a child and a third an elderly person. A third option might be to provide the children with a list of different parameters for the characters (wild animal, ghost, god, young boy, magician, eagle, would be just a few examples) and then ask them to select three ideas from the list and then leave them to make up a profile for each selection. This last strategy is an example of how providing a general framework, which does not impose detail, can help children to take ownership of the creativity – you have given them a helpful scaffold that supports their creative adventure.

You may feel it is beneficial for the children to write notes about each of the three chosen characters. If so, you could give them some headings to help structure their ideas. For example, a physical description, what they are wearing, any unusual behaviour or characteristics, how they talk (if they do), how they move, and so forth. However, you may not want to interrupt the children's flow with too much stopping and starting to write down ideas.

The group now possesses six or so different objects with unusual characteristics and three characters. Next, ask the group to invent a short, linked sequence of events that involves these components. This will be the dream narrative. The narrative might be written down in note form or more formally as a story or recorded on as a video or audio file, or simply remembered to be retold later.

Again, if the children have problems coordinating the narrative you could give them further guide ideas to help create flow. For example, there could be a problem to be solved, a journey to go on or a change that must take place.

The final product for the dream narrative could include a piece of imaginative creative writing. But, how about focusing, in this case, on an oral end product and ask each group to tell the whole class about their dream? This could be recorded and the children could transcribe their stories onto paper afterwards.

Creating dream paintings

This project uses the stimulus of the dream narrative the children have just created and includes preparing a simple 'story strip' to help children overcome problems both with selecting the subject matter and with the visual composition of their painting. Before you make a start it is worth asking yourself, 'Are there any specific painting skills that children might practise?' Alternatively, 'Do I need to teach the children any new painting skills, or do these skills need revising?' There are many different techniques for painting. For example, here are a few of the more straightforward questions that one might ask in reference to children's painting skills:

Are children able to mix their own colours?
Are they able to make a start, for example by planning the composition and setting out the image on the paper?
Are they used to using different sizes of brush?
Are they happy to make and then paint over mistakes?
Are they aware of the difference between using thick or watery paint?
Are they prepared to fill the picture area with colour?
Are they able to stop and go back to a painting, working slowly over a number of days?
Are they happy to build a painting in layers?

Are they able to select a technique for applying paint? For example, dashes and dabs or broad long brush strokes?

It would be impossible in one project, indeed in a host of projects, to teach children all possible skills. However, it might be worthwhile focusing on one or two to help improve the quality of the final product. In this project, we focus on a particular technique for planning the image: setting it out on paper using very pale paint and a thin brush. Then filling in colour areas with paint, letting these dry before enriching the painted surface by adding a second, more detailed, layer of oil pastel. First, children will need to create ideas for the composition. Here is one method that links up with ideas on creating narratives found in Part 1.

Fold an A2 sheet of paper in half and then in half again lengthways. Cut the paper along the folds to make four long strips. Give each child a strip and ask them to divide each strip into four, five or six sections. Give the children black note-writers, felt pens, coloured pencils and wax crayons to work with. They can choose which of these to use.

Ask each group of children to think about their dream narrative. Ask them to draw a sequence of events from the dream narrative in the sections along their strip. It might be helpful to tell them that they will be using one of these as the plan for their painting. This means that they should fill each section of strip with their drawing and not, for example, just draw along the bottom edge. You might ask them to add words, writing descriptions of the part of the dream narrative into the box. The children could use speech bubbles. In this way, if you choose, the project could become about drawing and writing comics. More about story strips and comics can be found in Part 1.

However, in this project our focus is on painting. After the children have had a chance to talk about their own and each others strips ask them to choose the one section which they would like to use as the starting point for a painting. You could help them by providing some guidelines to support their choice. For example:

Is there a background and foreground? Does the drawing fill up the section of strip? Is there action? Can you see clearly what is happening?

Will it be you or the children who decide on the size and shape of the paper for the painting? If it is the children you could have pre-cut a choice of say five different sizes and shapes to limit their choice and make it practical to manage. The shape of the paper may be dictated by the format of the strip segments the children have already used to plan their picture. Is it important that the rectangle for the painting and the rectangle of the segment are in the same ratio? It is best to use good quality cartridge paper or thin (non-glossy) card. The value of scrap card for painting on is often overlooked, if it is grey or brown and you would like a paler ground the children could give the card a coat of very slightly diluted white or pale matt emulsion to prime the surface before they start their painting. This will dry very quickly in a warm classroom. The children will need to transfer their drawing onto the surface that they have. For a description of a technique that you could teach the children to use, visit the appendix on page 150.

Creating a dream-like dance

This project might be clearly linked to the dream narrative and dream painting projects. Children could create a short dance that expresses the actions and emotions from a segment of the narrative they have already created on the paper strips. For example, their narrative may include ideas about sleep. Here, the teacher provides a framework that will help children structure and articulate their dance sequence focused on a specific idea that has been generated by the work up to this point.

This dance project begins with a warm up. For example, ask the children to begin by shaking their feet, then work around the body until each child is shaking hands, legs, arms, heads, fingers, shoulders... Now ask the children to stretch their toes and again, work around the body until each part has been stretched and relaxed.

Move onto ideas about sleep. Ask each child to pretend they are asleep but thinking about the position in which they like to sleep. For example curled up, stretched out, hand under head, on the left or right side. Ask the children to look at the different sleeping positions that the class has practised and to choose three contrasting ones including their own.

Now create the sleep section of the dance by asking the children to practise being asleep but changing the sleeping position, rotating from one position to the next every, say, five seconds. The children could experiment with the time delay between the movements, the speed of the change itself, gradual and sleepy or quicker and jerky as though disturbed by something. Review some of the children's sleep sequences with the whole class and ask the children to comment on how each sequence is different.

The central part of the dance is the dream sequence. This divides into three sections, entering the dream, the dream itself and leaving the dream. Ask the children to practise entering a dream dance by finding a way of getting up from the floor where they were enacting the sleep sequences but still appearing to be asleep. If this is difficult, give them some clues. For example:

Get up very slowly, act in slow motion, keep your eyes closed, tuck the head into their hands or arms as though they were asleep standing up, just act sleepy, think about how your body is after, say, a really long journey back from a holiday or after staying up all night.

Follow this with a short section of the dream narrative itself. The children can find ideas for the content of this from the dream narratives and the planning strips they made for the paintings. Although the work on the dance has been individual up to now, here, if you choose, the children can return to working in groups where each child in the group dances the actions or emotions of one character in one section of the dream, and then the characters can combine to dance together. Here is an example of how it might work:

Look at your planning strips for the dream painting. Pick a section. Choose one action or emotion that you would like to show. For example, in the dream your character might be climbing, falling, feeling angry or sad, running away, talking, arguing... What is your character doing or feeling?

Make up a dance that lasts no more than five seconds (count to five slowly while you are dancing) that shows the action or emotion you have chosen. Repeat this again and again, try and see if you can make it better and better.

Choose a second, different action or emotion and make up another short section of dance. If you like, work together in your groups to link up the dances with other characters. Maybe there is an action or emotion that you could all do together, in unison?

Photos: Roy Campbell-Moore, Diversions dance project, Cardiff

The children might use the objects that were collected for the start of the dream narrative project, if you or they felt they would be useful in the dance. You may remember that in our example on page 98 these included, a mobile phone, an alarm clock and a candle and each of these objects could help children devise dance movements to show actions. For example, lighting the candle, answering the phone, being surprised by a loud alarm.

In all passages of the dance, you can help children by suggesting they exaggerate movements, do them much more slowly than usual, emphasise contrasts and try to use as much of their body as they can.

The final sequence of the dance is leaving the dream to return to a deep sleep. The children could repeat, but in reverse, the actions described above in the paragraph about entering the dream. The children could return to the very first passage of dance asleep and changing rhythmically from one sleep posture to another.

The dance can now be practised and performed either by individual children or by one group at a time. You may be able to help children with refinements, such as the timing of the short sequences, the number of repeats of each mini-section and how to use the space in which they are performing to best show their dance, especially if they are working together. A group leader with a clap or other sound might signal changes from one section to another. This will help the group appear more coordinated.

A further option might be to ask each group to choose together one of the complete dance sequences devised by one of the group members. They all copy, learn, practise and perform it together, as a group.

Why not video the end product and take digital photographs to record the activity? Children could write a brief commentary, programme notes, which explain each part of the dance. These photographs could themselves form part of the raw material for the collage project that follows.

Teaching strategies

What are the strategies that underpin the teaching of this dream dance sequence? If we can extract them in general form they can be used to help both ourselves as teachers and children as creators understand how to build on the quite tightly controlled activity described above.

- Using ideas that have already been created by the group in a related activity, enhancing and sharing their meaning.
- Using the child's own experience to help devise the dance (in this example the child's experience of the postures adopted when asleep).
- Using spontaneous experimentation to help create the dance (children use their own ideas and see them valued).
- Division of the dance sequence into a small number of units (helps to create a structure that is more easily followed by the child).

- Keeping each individual dance passage short (less to remember, easier to practise and repeat).
- Creating patterns of movement through repetition (providing an aesthetically pleasing organisation, structure and so purpose to the dance).
- Reviewing and revising the dance movements themselves (improving and refining to improve quality).
- Performing, recording and acknowledging the finished performance.

This underlying structure could now be used to create new projects with an entirely different content. It is also possible to unravel when children have genuine creative choice inside the structure. For example, they can use their own experience, they can experiment spontaneously, they can decide on the length and number of repetitions, they can review and make changes, they can organise themselves in their group and decide on important features of the presentation and performance.

It is important to acknowledge that it is the teacher who has provided the structure and who remains in control of it. The teacher, however, does not need to dominate and control the content within this structure. It is here, safely inside the enclosed and comfortable precinct of a well-structured project, that children can begin to understand more about the process of creativity. »151

Dream collages

The dream collages project is designed to follow on from other projects in this section. For example, look back at the advice about creating a dream narrative or dream dance. They could also consider how combining ideas from their dream paintings might work in a shared dream collage. This project is designed for a group of, say, five children. But children could also work as individuals or in pairs.

This project begins with the children learning, revising and practising a skill. It includes possibilities for visual research using observational drawing, photocopying, scanning and a digital camera. It continues by exploring various ways of repeating and manipulating images using a photocopier (look back at page 97), the computer or the technology of scissors and glue. The collages could reflect dream narratives created by the group or reflect an understanding of dreams and dreaming from other cultures. The conclusion of the project is an exhibition of the finished collages and an annotated catalogue prepared by the children that will help a viewer interpret the dream.

It is helpful if children are able to use a technique for using glue with paper that will allow them to work in an organised way. Teachers could begin with a skills lesson that will show children how to organise their work space, how to apply glue, how to keep their work and their work space clean. Children could practise the technique they have learnt after having collected images during their research. For example, photocopy several images. Ask the children to cut them out using scissors and glue them on to paper. The aim is to allow them to practise a skill. Ask the children to suggest some statements that could be used to 'test' their skill. For example, 'there is no glue on the surface of the finished collage', or 'my work place was always tidy and well organised' or 'my images are well glued onto the background'. The children could also experiment by working onto these individual collages. For example, they could draw using, for example, felt pens or oil pastels.

The children will need to collect a bank of images for their collage. They could take digital photographs, make drawings, look on the internet, use CD ROMs, make photocopies from books and use images from magazines. The beauty of digital images is that they can be printed out or saved for later use or manipulation. Their own digital photographs can also be printed directly or saved onto the computer.

Children could be taught how to use the features of a photocopier to manipulate their images. Go back to page 97 to find out more about teaching children to use a photocopier. The image could be enlarged or reduced in size. They could transfer an A4 image to A3. They could darken or lighten the image. There may be other features on the particular machine in your school. These copier controls are not difficult to use and illustrate the way technology can be an integral part of the creative process.

Children could also be taught how to make simple image manipulations using software on the computer. For example, children can learn how to re-size images, crop images, apply filters that change the appearance of an image. They may go on to learn how to make the image lighter or darker. Does your software allow children to add text to the image? Children may digitally collage images. If the children are already familiar with image manipulation software they may be able to do much more. At some stage these digital images, manipulated or not, should be printed to add to the paper image bank.

One option is to include figures in the collage. These could be collected from magazines, enlarged and

manipulated in various ways if required. But if the children wish to include images of themselves, they could use digital cameras to take full length or portrait shots with different poses and expressions. A complete sub section of the project could evolve around this possibility. Consider the possibilities of face painting, costume and mime (look back at Part 1).

Children could also make observational drawings of the objects and images they would like to collect. This is a lengthier process but offers the teacher the opportunity to introduce a skills lesson on drawing. Drawing inanimate objects or copying images can be very dull but if this is seen by the children as part of a larger, more meaningful project, in this case, making dream collages, then they are far more likely to be engaged. When the observational drawings are finished. Make several photocopies or scans of each drawing, inviting the child to consider manipulating the image as before. »151

Whatever methods or combinations of methods are used, each group will have made a collection of images that are now printed or copied onto paper. These will be the raw material for the collage. These can be cut out ready to add to the collage. It is not always necessary to cut out the images with detailed care, going into every tiny corner with the scissors.

Each group will have a different idea about how strictly to relate the content of their collage to ideas from say, the dance, the dream story or other stimuli introduced by the teacher. Some groups will wish to create a largely illustrative collage, others will create more freely and the ideas expressed in the collage will be wider ranging. Both approaches are fine.

The groups can now work together laying out their collage. First, the teacher should explain that the collage is the initial stage and that after the images are glued in place the children will be able to add ideas, colours, patterns and so forth using different media such as felt pens, oil pastels and paint. Second, the children could continue to manipulate the paper images before they are glued to the collage by cutting, reassembling, re-copying and adding extra colour.

Third, the children can be helped to organise the collage. For example, give each group two sheets of paper or card, one is for the collage itself (there will be opportunities for the groups to choose the colour and size of the backing paper), the second sheet is used to layout the paper components of the collage so that they are able to see and adjust their visual ideas before they glue them down.

The discipline learnt or practised in the skills session at the start of the project will now be very valuable. If the group does not have enough space to work and to see their ideas clearly and are consequently in each others way and frustrated at not feeling in control, then the quality of the outcomes will be reduced.

To conclude the project, ask the children to talk to the class about their collage and the ideas that lay behind it. To illustrate the depth of content even more graphically for viewers and visitors why not take a digital photograph of each collage, crop to the edge of the collage to remove the background and print the image in colour. Glue this onto the centre of a much larger piece of paper and invite the children to annotate the image of their own work with written notes that describe the ideas, images, thoughts and feelings that their work expresses. »151

Dreams in other cultures

Children will have created and expressed many ideas of their own after working on the dream project. They will be excited to learn about how other people from other cultures express ideas about dreams, they will be curious about work by adult artists that can be linked to dreams. If you are now able to re-introduce children to expressions from different cultures, they will understand them better and they will mean more.

Dreams find many forms of expression. For example, are there paintings from western societies that you could introduce? Could you explore more deeply the role of 'dreaming' in the culture of indigenous Australians? You could tell them about other dreaming stories. Children might now be very receptive to examples of visual art from these Australian communities.

To widen their experience consider the fact that many other ancient cultures and indigenous tribes possessed a strong belief in the value of dreams. In China there were Dream Temples for the incubation of dreams. After special rituals of purification, you went to sleep to dream after asking for guidance for any problems you had. In Ancient Egypt, the people depended on their dreams to forecast the future. A great deal of literature exists about the Dreams of the Pharaoh. The earliest dream book ever discovered was created by the Egyptians in about 2000 BC. This dream book, called the Chester Beatty papyrus, includes over 200 interpretations. In Ancient Greece, people believed that dreams were divine, a gift from the gods. However, interpreting them could be confusing, because they also believed that dreams usually meant the exact opposite of what they seemed to mean.

To indigenous peoples all over the world, dreams are the focus of much of their thoughts and plans. And, in many tribes, the beliefs are similar – dreams are messages from the spirit world, whether from the gods, or from ancestors who have gone before. Dreams give advice and warnings. To some, the dreams are more real than reality. The Senoi are a small tribe of people who live in the mountains of Malaysia. They not only believe in dream symbolism, but also in total dream control. To return to western cultures, there are many examples of dreams and dreaming from cinema, both for adults and children. Are you able to think of any more examples from children's literature?

Why not conclude the project by gathering together some of this diverse and rich cultural information and associated images? Share these with children and ask their opinions about what they mean and the values they express. Is there a way that children could present both their own work and that of the various cultures they have encountered?

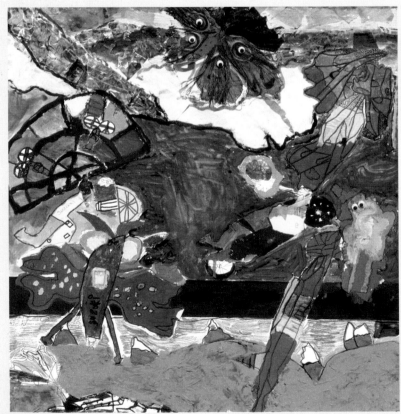

2.5
Imagination

Imagination is the process of creating a mental picture or an idea of something. Imaginings cannot exist, do not exist or do not exist here and now – although they are often predicated on past experience of reality. This capacity to picture or think something in the mind is part and parcel of the ability to create new ideas or scenarios. In the context of this book, these ideas can take concrete form through the arts, as imagination helps fuel creativity. All the projects in this book involve an imaginative response from children as they create something new.

This section suggests a project structure that could be adapted to many different subjects. It is illustrated with images linked to machines and animals. But teachers could equally focus on transport (cars, trucks, ships, aircraft), houses and homes (architecture, furniture, domestic appliances), engineering structures (bridges, skyscrapers, spacecraft), plants (trees, flowers), and natural environments (coral, gardens, the rain forest). The project structure could echo other sections of this book. Children could create imaginary people, clothes and toys. This is one form of the basic approach:

- Brainstorm or mind map ideas about the subject (for example, machines, flowers, bridges). Teachers can support children by guiding the principal questions and sub-sections of the subject that they are going to explore.
- Look at real world examples of the subject. This could involve library and Internet research, using a digital camera, photocopying images and drawing.
- Design an activity to focus on the parts or components of the real world subject.
- Consider creating an imaginary reason or context for the imaginary object. For example, a magical garden for imaginary flowers. Uses for imaginary machines. A society of imaginary animals.
- Reinvent an imaginary version of the subject, reassembling real world parts in different ways and/or assembling an imaginary object by imagining how new parts or components might look. Children could draw, collage or print various elements and parts.
- Can the children move on to make a sculptural version of their imaginary object?

Designing imaginary machines

In this project children will investigate machines in the real world in order to fuel imaginative ideas about their own inventive contraptions. The project is structured in such a way that children will create the context and therefore the significance of their work after looking at real machines. Begin by explaining that the children are going to create their own imaginary machines after they have collected and researched ideas about real machines.

What counts as a machine? For example, something mechanical or electrical that either does a task or helps us do a task? This would include domestic appliances. Which ever way you think about machines it might be good to start the project by brainstorming ideas about machines. You could ask them:

What machines help us go on a journey?
What machines help us at home or in the garden?
Do you know of any machines that help in the school?
Perhaps you could ask the adults at home if they use any machines at work.

Ask the children to use digital cameras to photograph different machines in and around the school. How many can they find? Next ask them to look do some research in the library. Can they find pictures of machines or parts of machines? They should be primed after the first activity to include a wide variety of objects. Make photocopies or scans of any images they find. All this visual material will be useful later.

Find a number of interesting looking machines for children to draw. Here are some ideas: take the back off an old television; draw the inside of a piano; bring in a mountain bike (concentrate on the gears). Find an old clock, a carriage clock for example; look inside the bonnet of a car. Take the back off an old computer or amplifier; look at a motorcycle. Find different kinds of machines in the kitchen. **»151**

The principles for a successful observational drawing activity are: plenty of talking about what they are drawing, a focus on one or more of the visual elements, the opportunity to practise before attempting a grand drawing and some guidance from the teacher about where to start, how to keep going without worrying about mistakes and when to finish. All this advice is available in detail on-line or in other publications, (you can can find more information in the appendix). The drawings are also going to be photocopied, so it is best to ask children to draw with something bold such as fibre tipped pens or note-writers so that the lines and shapes stand out and will photocopy well.

Ask the children to focus in on parts of the mechanisms. This can avoid the rather daunting task of drawing the whole of a complex object. Using view finders is one technique that children will find helpful. These are made by cutting a window in card and using this as a 'frame' to help isolate parts of a more complex subject. As you can imagine, if you have a number of different machines for children to draw, there will be a variety of drawings. Children can also draw the same object or mechanism from different view points of view.

Photocopy or scan the finished drawings. The originals can then be kept for display. Children will then have visual collections that include digital photographs, photocopies from books and photocopies of their own drawings. You could add printouts of images from the Internet to that list. Some of the most intriguing images could be photocopied several times. Look back at page 97 for advice about how to manipulate photocopies.

Before the next phase of the work, you could ask children to identify different elements of machines. In other words, can children begin to grasp the kinds of things that can go to make up a machine? Make a list of words that come up. Here are some ideas of what you might expect: cogs, gears, wires, metal shapes, grills, frames, fans, cable, containers, screws, bolts, clips, plastic covers, screens, levers, handles, buttons, chains, motors, circuit boards.

Ask children to work in groups. Why do they need a machine? It is at this stage of the work that you could link in to other projects in this book. For example, look forward to the work on creating political parties and their policies (page 127). Are there any problems in a community or in the environment that a new machine could help solve? Look back to the ideas linked to dreams. What could a machine do or be used for in a dream? Look back to Part 1 of this book. Is there work to be done or problems to overcome as children imagine life in their communities on an imaginary island? Ask each group to come to with a number of different machine ideas. Individual children can choose their own favourite idea or they could collaborate on ideas about one machine for the group.

The machine designs can be drawn or collaged. Children can cut out parts of machines from their photocopies, whether these are from photographs, their own drawings, print outs from the Internet or photocopies from books. This collage material can be rearranged and reassembled and then glued using a glue stick. Invite children to add extra drawn elements that are difficult to cut out or to find. They can draw over the top of their collages to add in detail or a background. »151

Drawings can be inspired by asking children to make up their imaginary machine by copying different machine parts from different photocopies and images in their collection. Or ask them to go free style, inventing all the various parts of their machine from scratch and only copying from the visual resource collection if they want to. Some children will enjoy annotating their drawings with notes and explanations. In this case, their drawing could look a bit like wacky illustrations from a manual. However, these drawings could also be finished in colour, with backgrounds and other details (the machine operators for example). Children could use paint and oil pastels.

If you think children are going to find it difficult to fit their collage or drawing to the paper, or that they are finding it difficult to know where to start, it can be helpful to suggest that they think about the middle of the machine first, placing the appropriate collaged or drawn element in the middle of their paper, gluing it down and then gradually 'building' the machine from there. Challenge children to work on a large scale. This is also a good activity for group work. Children can work together, combining ideas about an imaginary machine and go on to help each other make large drawings.

Making an imaginary machine

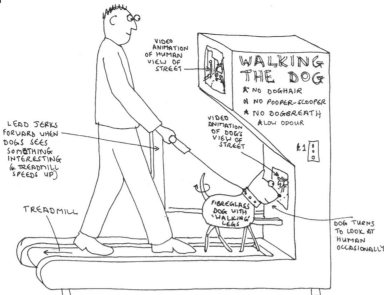

Rent a dog
Tim Hunkin, 2004

Labels in the illustration:
- VIDEO ANIMATION OF HUMAN VIEW OF STREET
- WALKING THE DOG
  - ★ NO DOGHAIR
  - ★ NO POOPER-SCOOPER
  - ★ NO DOGBREATH
  - ★ LOW ODOUR
- VIDEO ANIMATION OF DOG'S VIEW OF STREET
- LEAD JERKS FORWARD WHEN DOGS SEES SOMETHING INTERESTING (& TREADMILL SPEEDS UP)
- TREADMILL
- FIBREGLASS DOG WITH 'WALKING' LEGS
- DOG TURNS TO LOOK AT HUMAN OCCASIONALLY
- £1

Begin this mini project by asking children to experiment. There are quite a few different possibilities, here are two exercises that could build one on another:

How many different ways can each group find to join two pieces of paper or card together? Here are the tools and equipment you can use. We have, scissors, masking tape, Sellotape, glue sticks, hole punches, paper clips, treasury tags, strings and cords and a stapler. Don't forget that you can make slits and slots in the paper or card. Don't forget that you could fold or pleat the paper or card.

For the second example:

Your challenge is to find as many different ways as you can to make join three different pieces of paper and card together so that they stand up. I am going to show you how to use the scissors to score the card to help it fold well. You can also think about how to make supports for floppy or weak sections. Use the some of the techniques that you discovered in the first experiment but this time think in three dimensions!

Children could go on to make an abstract sculptural construction using the experiments. Ask each group to combine the experiments into a single construction. How is a larger construction going to be self supporting?

To make a machine, first ask children to draw the largest and most significant shapes of the individual parts of their machine onto flat card. If they have been looking at and talking about machines these shapes are quite likely to be frames, cases, containers and structures that support the smaller parts. Cut these shapes out and use them as templates so that the children can draw around and then cut out a second, identical shape to the first one. In other words the children are now going to have two flat shapes for each of the main parts of the machine. Ask them to think about each of the shapes as the sides of the main parts. Now they can use strips of card to join the two sides of each identical shape together. This will make them three dimensional. How are they going to assemble the main parts of the machine so that it is free standing? They can use the techniques that they will have discovered in the preliminary exercises.

Once the main parts of the machine are assembled. Children can add in smaller parts such as cogs, circuit boards, cables, wires, control panels and anything else that they can think of. Their sculptures could become quite complicated. Sometimes several hands are needed to hold and help. Children could work in twos or threes, either sharing the task of making a machine or working individually but stopping to help each other when needed.

The final constructions can be spray painted (normally this will need to be done by an adult). This will create a homogeneous effect making the machine seem to be made of one material. This can make the machines look more sculptural. An alternative is to paint or colour the parts of the machine before they are assembled. In either case children could use marker pens to add drawn details.

Many artists have been inspired by machines. For example, Eduardo Paolozzi created strange dream-like machines. These sometimes have human elements. Introducing work by an artist can expand possibilities in children's art. For example, the projects in this section could include the use of human forms metamorphosed into machines or suggestions of machines for specific tasks, informed by Paolozzi's art. Leonardo Da Vinci was an artist and engineer. A collection of drawings of his designs for machines is housed in Italy's National Museum of Science and Technology (Museo Nazionale della Scienza e della Tecnologia). Search their web site for images and ideas. Take the project into a mechanical theme as in Leger's Mechanical Elements. Children would enjoy seeing images of sculptures by Jean Tinguey, a twentieth century Swiss artist. Use a Internet image search to find examples of his work

Tim Hunkin is a UK based artist who has made small and large scale mechanical sculptures; children will enjoy his offbeat humour. At the time of writing you can find plenty of information and images on www.timhunkin.com.

Imaginary animals

Look back at the outline description of a generalised project structure on page 108. Here is a version of a similar structure that could be used to design an imaginary animals project.

- Brainstorm animals, make word lists of all the different kinds of animals children can remember.
- Research animals. Make a collection of many different images of animals and parts of animals. Look in the library and photocopy illustrations. Look on the Internet, print up useful images. Are there any CD ROMs in school? Perhaps one group could focus on insects, another on fish and so forth.

- Now brainstorm parts of animals. Children could think about the animals they have already suggested or found in their research. For example, snails and tortoises have shells, insects may have antennae, think about all the different kinds of wings, anteaters have long noses, elephants have trunks and crabs have pincers!
- Ask children to make a sheet of drawings of parts of animals. This is an excellent opportunity to revise the visual elements of shape and line. They could also add in markings and textures like scales, fur and skin. Children could annotate the drawings.
- Now ask children to work together in groups. Ask them to think about possible answers to questions such as these. Can they create an imaginary animal? What would it look like? What would it be called? Where does it live? What is its habitat like? What does it eat? How does it eat? What does it sound like? How does it move? How does it behave? Does it live with other animals in a community, herd or shoal? What are the main dangers the animal faces?
- Now each child can draw their version of the animal the group creates or they could go on to create and draw an imaginary animal of their own.

For stage two of the project, children could work together. They have already created imaginary animals, now these creatures can interact, communicate and form the principal characters in a story.

Look back at pages 41 and 42 for ideas about how to create narrative. In this case, the characters already exist. Look back at page 100 and use this technique to plan an imaginary painting or drawing using story strips. Advice about making a painting is found on page 150. The imaginary animals could feature in comics (page 146), in animations (page 48), children could make animal masks (page 66), create a dance based on animal movements (page 102), they could form communities (page 35) and even have their own sets of beliefs and political ideas as in George Orwell's *Animal Farm* (see also pages 118 and 127).

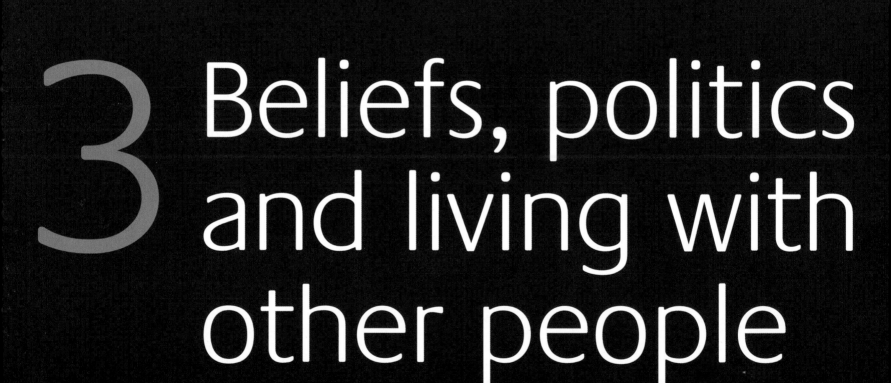

3 Beliefs, politics and living with other people

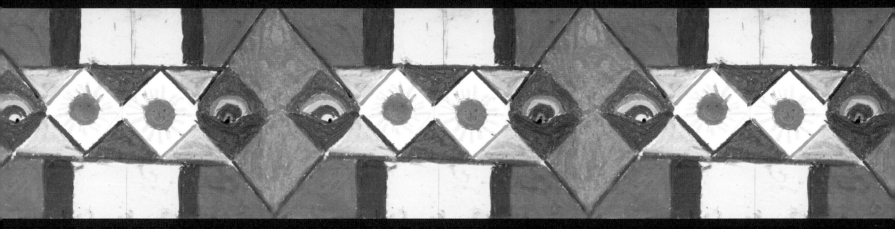

If you have been reading this book sequentially,
you will have travelled through ideas about creating
communities and imaginative cultures as well as
ideas about individual identity and imagination.
These two essential forces of human life, the self
and the group, are developed further in Part 3.
Communities are also societies, peopled by
individuals who have beliefs, who care about issues
and want to find ways to live with other people.
Children enjoy recreating imaginary versions of the
adult world through play. These imaginary worlds
can be quite complex. Consequently, the teaching
strategies in Part 3 explore ideas about belief
systems, ceremonies, art and architecture inspired
by spiritual and political issues, the needs of
communities and opportunities to make art
for other people.

Religious belief has inspired much art made by peoples throughout the world and throughout history. Imagine the power of Christian images of Christ or of heaven and hell, or the great iconic Buddha, or the animal masks of a spiritual ritual in an animistic society. This art is intensely meaningful to those who make it and those who see it.

Today, particularly in the West, societies happily appropriate images from wherever for whatever, stripping them of significance, recycling them for decoration and thereby mixing, muddling and confusing meaning. Not that this is all bad. In art and design the results are often visually exciting; we are breaking down boundaries between cultures and our lives are now richly decorated with visual references from all over the world.

In the primary classroom too, children are often asked to look at, record and recycle visual imagery from other cultures in their own work. They might decorate a clay tile with a fragment of Islamic pattern, or use the kinds of visual ideas about faces found in art from West Africa to make their own masks. Children draw from architecture, and mimic the dash and dab technique of French Impressionist painters. Although they are being introduced to art from around the world, it is often in a quite superficial way (critics call it tokenism). They sometimes use the visual motifs with little reference to their original significance and meaning.

This section explores strategies that draw out the qualities of meaning and significance that can inhabit spiritual or religious art. It does this by inviting children to create their own imaginary tenets of belief and even their own faux societies and belief systems. It invites children to consider meaning and significance at the forefront of their own creativity. It is hoped that children and their teachers may then go on to understand more about spiritually significant art from cultures other than their own.

3.1
Belief systems

Introducing children to beliefs

What happens when we discuss different kinds of spiritual beliefs with children? Can we help children understand more about different kinds of belief and help them respect the different meanings and deeply held convictions that underpin religions different from their own?

The activity that follows is one way of introducing children to the idea that there are different kinds of religious belief. By showing children simplified examples of different tenets of belief rather than telling children what a belief is, they grasp more quickly an intuitive idea of what we mean by belief in the context of this project. Ideas about where we come from, the possibility of god, the idea of different kinds of god and the possibility of the spiritual fascinate children. What is good and bad, what happens when we die, our relationship to the natural world or how to worship are just examples of powerful talking points.

To start with, why not ask the class what they already know about different religions? Do they know the names of any religions? Do they know about any religious festivals? What is a religion?

Teachers could make a number of sets of cards. In each set, the name of the religion is printed on the front and on the reverse one of the tenets of that religion. For example on a card about Buddhism you could type: 'What makes us unhappy is wanting too much pleasure. We always want more. To be content we must give up this craving for pleasure and enjoy what we have.' Alternatively, 'You must not hurt or think badly about anyone and you must not harm living creatures.' A card from a set about animist beliefs may say, 'Animals, plants, and the stars, sun and moon have spirits.' A card with an Islamic belief could say, 'Prayer must be done five times a day (upon rising, at noon, in mid-afternoon, after sunset, and before going to sleep) towards the direction of Mecca. The call to prayer is sounded by the Muezzin (Muslim crier) from a tower (a minaret) within the mosque.' It will be necessary to write out the tenets in a language suitable for the age of the children and with respect to their religious background. You could include beliefs and practices from any religion including, Hinduism, Sikhism, Judaism and Christianity as well as those religions already mentioned in this paragraph.

Place the children in groups of five or six. Each child chooses a card from one of the six packs. Each child should read out the text to the group. Ask them to talk about what each belief means.

Do you know what the sentence means?

Have you any questions about what is written on your card? For example, are there any words you don't understand?

Look on the other side of the card to see which religion the belief belongs to.

The groups could talk amongst themselves about the religious tenet written on the card. Alternatively, gather the whole class together and talk about some of the different tenets, what they mean and what religion they come from. It might also be helpful to have other teaching aids to hand, such as a map showing where different religions are practised or perhaps short video clips and photographs of people worshiping or preaching, or perhaps of people celebrating or marking important life events from each different religion. However, this is only a general introduction and the most important part of this activity is that children come across the different beliefs and talk about them. It is during this activity that they will begin to grasp what a religious kind of belief might be.

Creating imaginary beliefs

We can now invite children to create imaginary tenets of belief. This task may work best if the children have already invented an imaginary society (a community) for whom, these beliefs could be a vital part of the way they live. Accordingly, this project could also link well with the imaginary communities children invented in Part 1. The project is not difficult providing the teacher creates a structure to the activity. Children will create a quite complicated set of ideas as bit by bit they build understanding from simple components. What follows, suggests how a teacher might structure the creation of imaginary tenets of belief and an imaginary system of beliefs after children have created a kind of mini-society. Once these ideas are in place, they will provide a powerful and meaningful context for a range of artwork.

One way of starting the work is to ask children to invent imaginary people (see page 77) or tie this project in to the creation of imaginary communities (look back at Part 1, in particular page 35). Talking and sharing ideas about the imaginary people or communities will help to cement children's identification with what they have created and the meaningfulness of the ideas they are going on to create. For example, if the children have worked on large sheets of paper to draw imaginary people as suggested on page 62, try asking them to use these sheets as prompts to help describe their imaginary people to the whole class. Ideas can be both visual and written and the combination is very powerful. This is a useful skill and any set of ideas, in this case about people, can be described using both words and pictures.

Now ask the children to decide what their imaginary people or community believe. It may be helpful to revisit the tenets of belief from the first activity to remind children about the kinds of things that count as beliefs. Ask each group to create about four or five beliefs for their imaginary people or imaginary community. Remind them to think about what kinds of people these are. For example, if their community lives in trees and talks like birds what kind of god might they believe in? Or, do they think that they change into birds when they die (a kind of reincarnation)? Of course, a community that lives in an ultra-modern city in the future may believe that computers control the world. You can never turn a computer off because terrible things may happen if you do. These two examples give some idea of

where children may go with their ideas. Of course, some beliefs will be more straightforward. For example, that people should be kind to each other or that angels exist and are good. It might be that a characteristic of the imaginary community attains the status of belief. For example, everyone wears black because they believe in the power of black; or that because running fast is so important (to escape from lions or monsters) the imaginary people only pray whilst they are racing!

First of all talk in your groups and try to agree some sentences that describe a belief for your community. You will need at least four beliefs. It is best to write one sentence for each belief. Write these on these large sheets of paper using the marker pens. Ask a secretary to write down the beliefs that you have all agreed on. Use large writing so that other people can read your ideas clearly.

Pick someone from the group who will describe the imaginary beliefs to the whole class. Get them to practise in front of your group. Make some comments and criticisms so that they can improve what they are going to say and how they are going to say it. Then we will ask each group to describe what their community believes in.

The children could create a name for their mini belief system or imaginary religion. For example, a group that believed in the power of rainbow colours and worshipped colour created the name *Colourtism* for their imaginary religion. There is much to be talked about, shared and described. You could go back to ask children to pick over the detail of their beliefs and communities a little more. Where do they worship? Are there special ceremonies? Are there any stories or parables to be told? This kind of talk can lead neatly into the next phase, the art.

If you have followed the project up to now children will have invented imaginary people with particular characteristics and behaviours. Alternatively, they have created or revisited imaginary communities suggested in other parts of this book. These people have beliefs and these are formed into a kind of imaginary belief system. The projects that follow work because the children create art for their people and their beliefs that is meaningful in the context ideas they have created themselves. It has both content and purpose.

Designing religious motifs and patterns

Making a greetings card

Why not start this simple design project by showing children different examples of religious motifs and symbols and talking about their significance? Look forward to page 125 for examples of a few ideas about religious art, craft and design. One way of finding a range of motifs is to image search on Google. Make a small file for each religion and store the different designs for the children to view later. Clip art collections may also have a range of simple motifs.

Children could make their own drawings of these symbols and add written notes by way of explanation. Use sketchbooks or larger sheets of paper. Make a list together of different categories that the symbols fall into. For example, food, animals, household objects, natural things. Look back at page 35 for more detailed ideas about how to help children design a motif.

Next, introduce children to ideas about pattern. Again, this is covered in some detail from pages 34 to 38. There are many applications for pattern in design. Children could go on to use their patterns and motifs on clothing, fabrics, as part of architecture, in interiors, as part of printed material and as simple decoration. In this project, the patterns and motifs will have meaning inspired by the imaginary people, the communities and the beliefs they hold.

This is also an opportunity to use a computer to help repeat motifs or pattern designs again and again. Children can rotate and tessellate copied images. Computer designs such as these can be printed and used as part of other design projects.

Why not show children the kinds of patterns that have religious significance or are used in a religious context? Teachers can interweave ideas and images from other cultures into this project or devise new work spinning out of the ideas encountered in this section so far.

Fold A4 card in half to make an A5 card. Children can also have A4 paper folder to A5 for practice. The image could be inspired by a motif, pattern, ceremony or story linked to the children's imaginary beliefs. The card could be made using traditional graphic media together with computer generated text and images. The project can involve the graphic design of both the image and text for a greeting or message inside. The text could be 'typeset' using normal word processing software. This could be printed out and collaged to the inside of the card.

Children could help select the best designs and textual ideas, short listing designs and then voting in class. Commercial printing can be surprisingly inexpensive. Ask two or three printers to quote for printing one or more of the cards. Some printers offer a service via the Internet. However, if you choose a local printer, this is a perfect opportunity to take children to visit the printing press and follow the process of seeing their visual ideas transferred via technology to the finished card. The idea that printing allows the same image to be repeated again and again is a fundamental concept in art and design; so perhaps you would prefer children to print a greetings card in class. They can block print or use the specialist polystyrene blocks available from educational suppliers. Inviting an artist into school to help with technique offers the children a chance to learn about printmaking from a professional, whilst at the same time working with their own visual ideas. The cards with their messages can be sent to family and friends at important times of year, or simply used to celebrate a festival or commemorate an event for the children's imaginary community. »151

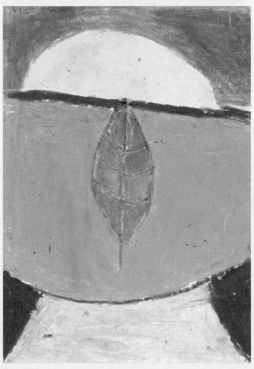

Architecture and places of worship

If children have followed the kinds of activities suggested by this section, they will have developed a strong sense of their imaginary beliefs. They may also have created a visual identity expressed through motifs, patterns and, possibly, designed objects and artefacts. Teachers may have introduced children to a number of world religions and looked at some of the appropriate symbols and patterns. The opportunity to create imaginary ceremonies, celebrations, festivals and ways of worship now presents itself. However, before we consider these ideas, perhaps children would enjoy designing and making a place of worship. Here is a brief outline of a possible project structure.

- Collect images of places of worship from a number of different religions to show the children. Talk about how people worship and how the buildings show various aspects of religious belief and practice (for example, minarets on mosques and Buddhist prayer flags on temples and spires pointing to heaven on churches).
- Ask children to make a collection of architectural details from various images. For example: different towers, window shapes, entrances, roof structures, pattern and decoration. Children should only be drawing parts of the buildings.
- Now ask children to repeat this exercise only this time drawing imaginative features. Ask them to link the architectural details they draw with their imaginary religion and the people or the community who practise it. For example, a religion focused on beliefs about the sea may have a building (or an undersea grotto) with windows, and doorways in the shape of fish.

- Invite children to draw a complete design. This could be a façade, or perhaps there could be a number of different views. To help children get started, suggest that they begin their design in the middle of the paper adding various elements of the building until they have exhausted their ideas.

- Children can draw lightly in pencil. When they are happy with the drawing, they can draw over the pencil lines with felt and handwriting pens. They can add colour and any additional details. For example, have they remembered items like, locks, drainpipes, steps, roof tiles, trees and plants around the building?

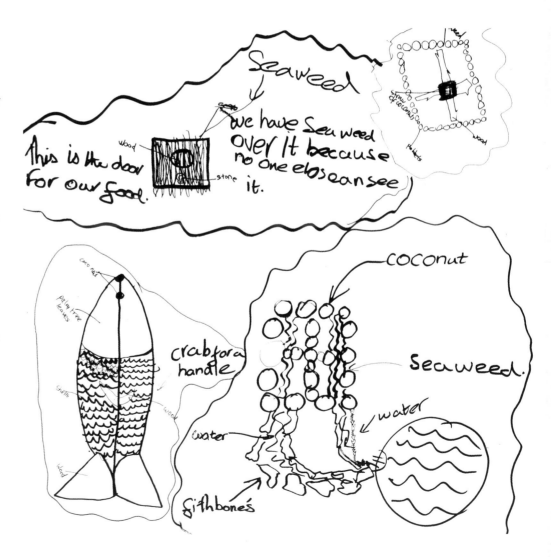

Making an imaginary place of worship

If you prefer, children can move onto construction without necessarily drawing out a complete design first. There are advantages and disadvantages with either approach. If children make too detailed a design, they may become frustrated and disappointed at the difficulties of a construction that fails to match an ambitious design. In addition, the project could become too extended, testing their endurance. However, if children construct without first developing ideas in design terms, the products might be poorer, in terms of both idea and technical achievement.

A compromise could be to allow children to create the imaginary parts of a place of worship on paper (for example, door and window ideas). They could then experiment with the kinds of techniques that will be useful in the construction before making the imaginary place of worship. Look back at page 111 where there are a number of ideas about how to help children explore construction with paper and card. For this project, they could also use thin strips of wood and dowel, art straws, pre-cut strips and lengths of thick card such as grey board and junk cardboard from boxes and packaging. The activity on page 111 describes ideas about joining. To extend the children further you could design a preparatory activity that explores the idea of jointing.

Children will find it much easier to work together on the construction and it is likely that they will have created ideas about imaginary beliefs in groups (see page 118). Supply a large sheet of stiff card or thin plywood as a base so that the constructions can be easily moved out of the classroom. Begin by talking about the experiments and discussing the kinds of methods of joining and jointing that are going to give the structure strength. For example, rolling paper into tubes creates columns; making joints with triangles will help make a geometric construction stronger; using ties, stays and supports can help with balance. Suggest that some children concentrate on making details such as individual doorways and windows. These can be directly inspired by their imaginative drawings. Also, inevitably, children will be influenced

by images of real places of worship from different world religions. However, the constructions may not be buildings. After all people could worship in forests, by pools, under waterfalls and at sea!

As the constructions develop, teachers could supply additional materials. For example, a box of bits and pieces such as plastic packaging, coloured cellophane, fake grass, twigs, moss, all kinds of wools, electrical wire and more.

An alternative or parallel approach could be to ask children to revisit any religious motifs and patterns they made earlier in the project. Can these be incorporated in any way as decoration or even as an integral part of the structure?

Are children going to include model figures? These can help show scale. A construction could include three immense forest trees. These have become a place of worship for a community of people who believe in tree gods. Without small figures, it will be difficult for the spectator to imagine the scale that children intend. Two-dimensional figures could be made out of card, three-dimensional figures out of clay. Look ahead to page 123 and the project about installations for a brief description of making small clay figures. If children have arrived at this project via other work that included creating imaginary people or an imaginary culture for an island community, these figures could be shown in appropriate costume. The finished constructions can now become the imaginary venues for the creation of ceremonies, the performing of chants and the setting up of shrines.

Ceremonies, chants and incantations

Children will delight in creating a ceremony that could have been performed in the imaginary place of worship. If they have been following the project described in this section, they will have created imaginary beliefs for imaginary people or communities, designed motifs and patterns and drawn or constructed a place of worship. Children will have a clear sense of the character of their beliefs. Why would there be ceremonies? Who are the ceremonies for? Where exactly will the ceremony take place? What will happen in the ceremony? What will people wear? What will people say, sing or chant? Ask children to brainstorm these kinds of questions.

A chant is the rhythmic speaking or singing of words or sounds, either on a single pitch or with a simple melody involving a limited set of notes and often including a great deal of repetition. An incantation is the words spoken during a ritual. Another name for an incantation is mantra. Chants, incantations or mantras are one of the simplest musical forms. Could children include a chant or incantation as part of the ceremony?

Here is a simple example of how to help children create a chant. First, lead children through an example. The structure of the task is as follows:

- Create a number of real or imaginary words that will make up the chant. For example, children could make a chant with the single words 'tree' and 'bird' or the imaginary words vjay and loy. In the first instance, use single unconnected words to keep the activity easy to follow. Chants that are more complex can be created later.
- Chose the pitches for the chant. Start by limiting the available pitches to say, E, G and A. Use a chime bar or glockenspiel to help children identify the pitches for the chant. Later they could choose their own.
- Fit one of the words or a syllable to a pitch and continue until you have a simple melodic shape. For example, the word 'tree' could be extended over ten modulating pitches of A G and E. This means the word is sung unbroken as the pitch changes. For example, the word 'tree' might take 10 seconds to sing, with the 'ee' of 'tree' strung out over the changing pitches (say: G, E, G, A, G, E,

G, G, E – holding the last E, and followed by a pause, before repeating the line again). You can add different lines, using different words with the same three notes, not forgetting the potential of pauses. Why not use repeated lines?

- Now the children have words, pitches and a few different melodic shapes. They can now add a drone. In our example, use the pitches G and D. The drone can be sung or hummed by half the class as the other sings the chant, or it could be played on sustaining instruments, such as keyboards, violins or recorders.
- Different groups in the class could sing different lines simultaneously to create a layered effect.
- Musical children will learn quickly how to create their own chant. Less musical children (and adults) will need to work in groups and have support.

To notate the chant you could use a simple series of letters or symbols. Children could create their own simple visual musical notation for their imaginary religion or community.

The ceremony

This project could bring together a number ideas. Look back at: page 65 for ideas about costume; page 57 for ideas about printing fabric (in this case, the fabric could have a religious meaning and be used as part of the ceremony in the form of banners, hangings, cloaks and so forth); page 55 for ideas about decorating ceramic objects that might be used in a ceremony; pages 53 and 102 for ideas about a dance; page 42 for ideas about creating a myths (for example, a story could become a parable to read out during the ceremony); and page 51 about creating a song. Children could also consider creating a shrine (or other special, spiritual, place) where the ceremony is to take place. Children might imagine their ceremony in their imaginary place of worship. Teachers can support children in bringing all or some of these possible strands together. The end product is an enactment of the ceremony, which could include statements about beliefs, the community and presentations of the various visual and cultural elements.

Shrines, installations and the significance of objects

A shrine is sometimes the innermost sanctuary of the temple where objects, icons and sculptures are placed, which has deep significance for religious beliefs and practices. Teachers could introduce children to the idea of shrines by revisiting world religions. For example, a Shinto shrine is where the Kami, the Shinto gods live. Sacred objects are stored in shrines. For example, children might come across: Komainu, a pair of guardian dogs, lions, or foxes that are often found on each side of a Shinto shrine's entrance. A purification fountain is found near the entrance. Visitors are supposed to clean their hands and mouth before approaching the main hall. Omikuji are fortune telling paper slips found at many Shinto shrines and temples. Visitors choose a paper slip at random; they contain predictions ranging from daikichi (great good luck) to daikyo (great bad luck). By tying the piece of paper around a tree's branch, good fortune will come true or bad fortune can be avoided. Shrine visitors write their wishes on Ema (wooden plates), and then leave them at the shrine in the hope that their wishes will come true. Most people wish for good health, success in business, passing entrance exams, love or wealth. Teachers can research more about Shinto on the Internet to give children information about the main beliefs and how the shrines reflect these. Researching a particular example such as this could help teachers structure a project that allows children to create original ideas of their own whilst, at the same time, learning how spiritual and religious ideas are expressed in other cultures. In this case, ask children:

What is going to guard your imaginary shrine?
What is kept in the your shrine?
Is there anything special you have to do before entering the shrine?
Think up a way of giving and receiving messages.
What kinds of objects or actions will bring good luck?

You could try the activity after they have created imaginary beliefs, but before you introduce them to Shinto shrines. Whichever style you choose, children can go on to create shrines for their own imaginary beliefs which could form a focal point for their ceremonies.

Ideas about the special significance of objects can also be developed in non-religious ways. Contemporary artists have used installations to present objects in juxtapositions and collections. Sometimes the objects are changed in some way, sometimes not. Video and photography are often included. The objects and the way they are displayed can often have an important significance for both the artist and the viewer.

Here are two examples. The first is an idea for an installation inspired by the idea of Omikuji the Shinto fortune telling paper slips described above. Brainstorm lots of different ways of displaying a single written phrase. For example:

How will the phrase be written? On the computer, with mud, in paint, very small?
On what should the phrases be written? Paper, cloth, ribbon, scrap, a white board, on a web site?
How many phrases could you all write?
How do think all the phrases be displayed or recorded?

Could the class think of an interesting way other people could experience discovering the phrases. For example, hang each phrase from a network of lines, staple each phrase onto specially printed fabric, hide each phrase in a pile of discarded objects, put each phrase in a sock and the socks in one pile, take the phrases onto the beach and bury them in the sand, tie each phrase to a helium balloon with the address of the school, will any return? Ask the children for their ideas. What could it mean, for example, to float away a wish on the wind? Ask children to talk about what their ideas might mean.

Next, brainstorm what children think they could write. For example, wishes, good thoughts, something beautiful, something bad, a horoscope, a belief. How might people who visit the installation react to the phrase? Could they write a phrase of their own? Could they take the phrase away and place it somewhere else? Could they draw a picture to go with the phrase and put it back into the installation? Could they read the phrase to a video camera? Why would people make an installation like this? Do the children think people would find the installation interesting? Once everything has been decided, provide children with the materials needed to first think up and then write their phrase. Invite another class to interact with the installation. Although these are examples of how the project might work, ask the children for their ideas before influencing their thinking too much with examples of your own.

The second idea is inspired by British sculptor Antony Gormley's installation called 'Field'. Gormley uses the human form to explore mankind's existence in, and relation to, the world. Field is a series of installations made in collaboration with communities from across the globe. Tens of thousands of small clay figures are made by members of a community, who might be from the USA, Indonesia or North Wales! There were a few rules: the figures had to be hand-sized, easy to hold, eyes must be deep and closed, and the head was to be in proportion with the body. Figures ranged in size from 8-26 centimetres tall, and were dried in the sun and then baked in a brick kiln. When the thousands of figures are placed close together in a great crowd, they could be seen as an invasion. Perhaps the sensation is that of a tide; an endless mass that completely fills the room and spills outside. In 1994 Antony Gormley was awarded the Turner Prize for Field, and he is also well known for his large outdoor sculpture Angel of the North near Gateshead on Tyneside.

Field for the British Isles
Antony Gormley
Installation Tate Gallery, Liverpool, 1993
Terracotta (approx 40,000 figures)
© the artist. Courtesy Jay Jopling/White Cube (London)

Teachers can find images of 'Field' on-line. The illustration shows 'Field for British Isles' from the Arts Council Collection. The idea of a crowd of simply made clay figures could inspire children. However, it might be better to use the idea of Field as a starting point for a class installation that adopts some of the ideas but allows children to take control over the meaning. For example, 'Field' suggests that a large number of similar objects or ideas shown close together has an aesthetic and emotional impact. Could children brainstorm an idea for an installation that has at its core the presentation a large number of similar or identical objects? What could this collection of objects mean? For example, what might be the effect of a wall completely filled with photocopied images of family members? To make this installation each child would need to contribute one or more snapshots.

These can be photocopied many times, children can roughly cut out images, hand colouring is a possibility, words and notes could be added and the hundreds of people can be collaged onto a single wall. This might be a reflection on vast numbers of people who are in all the families of everyone in the class. Perhaps the installation could be organised by having babies on one side which gradually merge to children then adults into images of older relations. How would the children choose to organise the images? Perhaps friends should be included. Children could use a digital camera or camera phone to photograph as many people they know as they can! Digital cameras are easy to use. How can teachers help children use them more thoughtfully? What are some of the underlying skills that children could learn? How can digital photographs be valued as art works in themselves?

On page 138 children took the photographs of their installations based on toys and the following section has more ideas about linking with issues-based contemporary art.

Religious art, craft and design

Hindoo Gods
Wallpaper, Allan, Cockshut
& Co. (manufacturer),
Victoria and Albert Museum

To conclude this section teachers can research and show children examples of religious art. The Internet offers a very effective research tool: there is a wealth of information and images about art from all the world religions. Most importantly, it is usually possible to link the art with the underlying beliefs of the relevant religion. Here are some examples of ideas that teachers could introduce to children.

Buddhist prayer flags are inscribed with symbols prayers, and mantras. Tibetan Buddhists display these flags outside their homes and places of worship. As the wind ruffles and blows the flags, prayers are, as it were, shaken and dispersed across the countryside. Prayer flags bring happiness, long life and prosperity to the flag planter and all those near by.

Icons have been a focus for Christian worship for nearly two millennia. Typically, there is a robed figure with fingers raised in a 'teaching' gesture, and clasping a book. This is an ancient image with origins in Greek, Roman and Egyptian cultures. An icon seeks to bring about an experience of stillness and constancy. The gaze of the image seems directed at the viewer in an intimate and personal way. Many people find that this helps them to identify spiritual and eternal qualities.

The Hindu god Vishnu looks after the universe; he is the embodiment of generosity. Religious images show Vishnu sleeping on the coiled serpent Shesha or Ananta floating in the cosmic ocean. He is always extremely handsome. Brahma (the Creator) appears in a lotus flower which rises from Vishnu's navel. Vishnu's sleep on the eternal waters symbolises the dormant periods between the ages of the universe. Brahma's reappearance signals his re-creation of the universe to begin a new age.

Children who have experienced creating beliefs, imaginary religions, places or worship, shrines, chants and ceremonies will be very receptive to finding out about how real people have created religious art. Each of these three ideas (and there are many, many more) could prompt new artwork.

3.2
Politics and living with other people

Politics is the process by which a community's decisions are made and through which rules for group behaviour are established. People choose leaders to make decisions. These leaders have power. To a greater or lesser extent, this power is dependent on being able to convince people that the leader's judgements are good and in the people's best interests. The people may replace leaders if they appear to take consistently poor decisions. In democracies, leaders have to convince people that their ideas will work. In this way, politics acts as a catalyst for the discussion of issues. Groups and individuals argue or campaign for this policy or that policy in response to an issue.

Power, decisions, making rules or laws. Ideas about how we can best live in groups and communities with other people. How we think as individuals and how that effects our attitudes to others. The issues that are uppermost for leaders and people; issues that affect us as individuals. This is the stuff of politics. If you look back through this book, you will find a number of sections that could precede the work we are embarking on here. For example, imaginary islands, imaginary worlds or imaginary city communities; imaginary personalities, as they come together in a community; imaginary animals and how they might live together. In Part 3, you may have already found ideas about creating imaginary sets of beliefs.

As this is a book about art, the process of politics is not to the fore. Rather, it is the expression of ideas about *issues* that fuels much adult art and that will also engage children as well as give meaning to the work they do. However, before we look at art about issues, the following project is designed to help children understand a little bit about the idea of politics, if only that people come together take decisions and to argue and campaign for issues.

Creating an imaginary political party

A political party is a group of individuals who share roughly the same ideas about issues that affect our lives. They often try to win power through election. Because of this, they have to convince other people of their ideas. Some political parties are only interested in one issue, so they put all their energy into convincing people that this big special issue is important.

Children may already have come together to create imaginary communities or created sets of beliefs. If so, teachers could use this previous work as a starting point. What problems could the community have? What does the community need to decide? Here is a possible list of questions for brainstorming, discussion or mind-mapping:

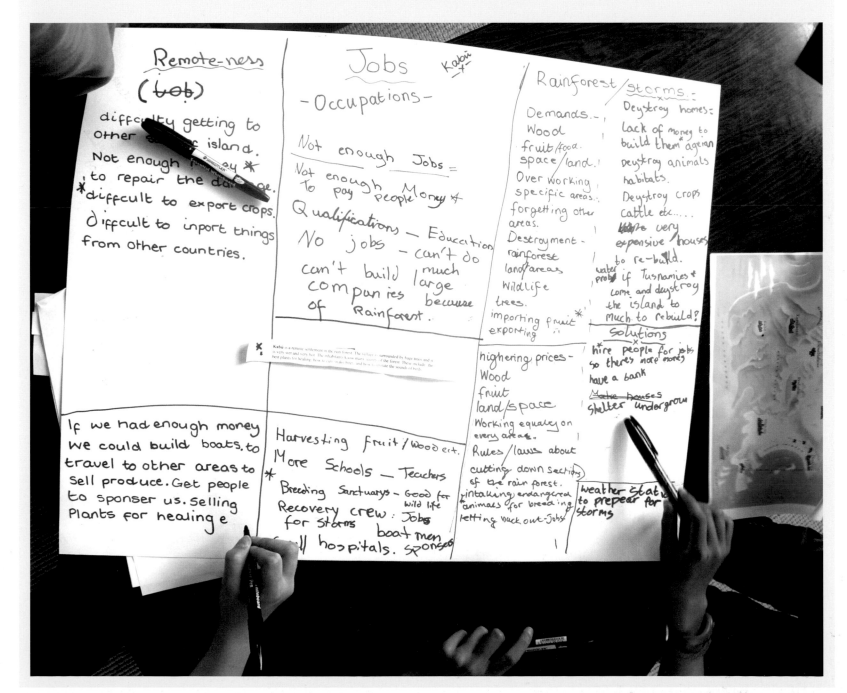

Could there be problems with food? Has everyone enough to eat?
Are people healthy or is there a problem with illness?
Has the community enough money? Why does it need more money?
How does the community spend its money? Why?
Should the community spend its money on different things? What are the priorities?
Is there enough work for people to do?
Are there poor people? What are their problems?
How do children learn? What do children learn?
Are there problems with other communities?
Is the community in danger? What does it do to protect itself?
What happens when people get old?

There are many more such questions and each issue above could be subdivided. For example, food:

Where does the food come from?
Where and how is the food stored?
Who is in charge of the food?
Is there enough food?
What different types of food does the community need?
What happens when there are shortages?

Alternatively, work:

Where do people work?
What is the work like?
Are people paid? Is it enough?
Do people get time off? When?
What happens if there is too much work?
What happens if there is too little work?

As politicians deal with almost every aspect of community life, then these questions could be endless. Teachers will be able to help children focus on specific issues, depending on how they see the outcome developing.

Teachers can now help children identify the ideas that they think are most important. For each issue they could state a problem, what caused the problem and then what they would do about finding a solution. For example, there is not enough food. Why? Because they live near a desert and there is not enough rain. Solution. Campaign to dig a canal to bring water from a lake. What's the problem with this idea? Another community that lives near the lake is against the idea. They are worried that the lake will dry up. Another example. Everyone is bored. Why? There is not enough work to do and there is nowhere to go to have fun. Solution. Build a factory near the village where people can work. What's the problem with this idea? The village is lovely just the way it is and the factory will be ugly.

As you can imagine there is an infinite variety of issues, problems and solutions. When each group has thought through which issues they are going to focus on, they can create a political party to campaign for them. The idea is that they will have to win enough votes to get elected so that they can take the decisions they think will solve the problem.

Here are some ideas about creating an identity for the political party:

What is the name?
Can you design a motif or logotype for the party? (Look back at page 35 for ideas about motifs).
What is the party's colour (or colours)?
Is there a leader? Who is the leader? (Look back at page 78 for ideas about creating an imaginary personality, or the children could choose one of themselves as a leader).
Design a poster about one of your issues (see the next project).
Design a leaflet with text and images that explains who you are and what your policies are.
Design an advertisement for a newspaper.

Each group can prepare a presentation to the class about their party and the issues they think are most important. They can distribute pamphlets, show the poster and make a speech. Ambitious projects could include a party political broadcast (on digital video) or a computer-aided presentation.

After all the presentations, questions to each of the political parties and a general discussion, all the children in the class can vote in a secret ballot (but not for their own party). Which party gets the most votes? To make it more interesting there could be a first, second and third choice on the ballot paper. As an alternative, there could be three rounds. In the first round, the two parties with the least votes drop out. In the second round, the party with the least votes drops out leaving a final round to be contested by two or three parties. A chance for them to try to convince the electorate one more time!

Designing a political advertisement

This could be a poster, newspaper or magazine advertisement, leaflet or a short video. Children will be very motivated by this kind of project. The art work that results will be meaningful for them and they are likely to be more committed to it. Teachers may like to search around for ideas. For example, at the time of writing in April 2005 the American Museum of the Moving Image has an on-line exhibition devoted to political television commercials in the USA. There are also links to other resources for teachers. There are many images of political posters on the Internet. For example, try a search for 'political poster' or 'political advertising'.

Posters

Children will benefit from some simple guidelines. You can make some of the choices clear to them. Keep the image simple. Use interesting text. Think about appropriate colours. The main image could be drawn, painted, collaged or photographed. Text could be computer generated using different fonts (but not too many), font sizes and the application of effects such as bold, italics and colour. However, text could be hand-painted or drawn. The entire poster could be made on a computer by adding text to an image using a paint or graphics package.

The photocopier could be a very useful. Look back at page 97 for advice about using a photocopier to metamorphose images. Collage will be a valuable technique. For example, children could generate text on the computer, print it out and collage it onto an image. Hand drawn and painted elements could be combined with collaged photographs.

Children could use a digital camera to take their own photographs. For example, they may decide to feature a photograph of their leader on the poster. If you look back to page 65, there are ideas about costume. The photographs can be printed and enlarged on the photocopier. Black and white photocopies could be hand-coloured. Perhaps the election poster includes a photograph of the party leader in traditional costume! The work on textile design could prompt children to make a banner or flag. The group could work as a team. For example, two children could work on the poster. Two more on a leaflet and another two on an advertisement for a newspaper or magazine.

our aims:
Education, *not destroying the rainforest,* **more jobs,** more children go to school, *re-build* homes after storms, **Education,** *not* destroying the rainforest, joining the recovery crew, *boats for transport,* wild life sectaries, under ground shelters, *Education*

Campaigning about issues and promoting your community in print

Teaching children about politics is helpful if they are to understand how communities and societies function. For example, how people come together to take decisions and solve problems, and how issues about the way we live together are defined and expressed. Art and design has a valuable part to play. For example, children can promote their communities using printed media and graphic design. The illustrations show examples of leaflets that talk about housing, employment, the economy, transport, cuisine, recreation, tourism, festivals, and beliefs.

What would you like to tell people about your community? How could you attract tourists or people to come and live in your community. Could you attract businesses to come and invest in the community and create jobs?

Could children organise a campaign to fight for an issue their community believes in? For example, protecting the environment and saving endangered species. More often than not, adults mount displays in the classroom. Could children take control over a display area and put up a display or presentation about their campaign without help from the teacher? As part of the campaign children could design T-shirts, badges, leaflets, posters and adverts in print and for television.

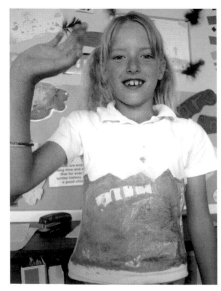

Television interviews

Look back at page 46 for ideas about presenting a news item. This basic advice is useful for this project too. This project explores interviews on camera. Children can prepare questions and answers based on the ideas of their political party and the issues on which they would like to focus.

Divide the groups into politicians and reporters. The reporters have to think up questions for other politicians in other groups. The politicians have to revise what they would like to say about their issues. Each group will already have heard ideas and seen posters, leaflets or advertisements from the other political parties. Nevertheless, it might be wise to confirm the subject matter that the reporters will be asking questions about, so that both politicians and reporters can prepare.

Children find this activity much easier if they can hold a microphone. The action of first holding the microphone to your own mouth when asking a question and then reaching out with the microphone, holding it just underneath the politician's mouth, helps everyone know when to start and finish speaking. The microphone can be connected into a socket on the camera, but be sure to have the camera on a tripod and a long enough lead for the microphone.

Children will need to choose or set up a background to the interview. Is there good light? They will usually look and feel more relaxed standing up rather than sitting. There could be a camera operator, a sound engineer, a lighting engineer and a director as well as the politician and the reporter (look back at page 128).

It is probably best if the interviews are conducted without the normal background chatter in a classroom.

You could try the activity twice. The first time around no one has a chance to practise answering and asking questions on camera. They have to do the interview spontaneously. Play back the results, talk about how they could be improved and ask the children to practise before having another go. This first attempt is more spur of the moment and realistic, but will be full of faults. Children will learn a lot by being able to see how they can improve the second time around.

The following ideas may help groups develop a classroom television news programme based on interviewing a politician. Each reporter prepares the questions she wants to ask and decides on the order. You could plan a 'set' for the interviews or simply make them outside 'on the street'.

The reporter could introduce the subject and the politician by giving some background before he starts asking questions. The reporter will need to prepare this. Programmes that are more complicated will need a storyboard but this project is simpler. However, the children could make their own cue cards with marker pens.

Interviewers should ask the politician what they would like to be called on camera and remember it. They could also talk to the politician in advance to warn them about the questions they are going to ask. However, some fun can be had with reporters asking surprise questions! Even questions that have nothing to do with the subject! Allocate roles – camera, sound, lighting, and director. Look back at page 46 for more advice.

Reporters, start by writing out in note form a list of the questions which you would like to ask. If you are doing, for example, an interview about shortage of food in the desert town you could include three main questions:

- *Why isn't there enough food in your village?*
- *How are the people reacting?*
- *What is your solution to the food shortage?*

You only need to write out your first question in full. Make notes about your other questions. Make a cue card if you can't remember your next question. But you will find as the interview continues that you may change what you ask because of what the politician has already said. If you do this your questions will sound natural and spontaneous.

Having the questions in note form also stops you rehearsing the next question to yourself when you should be listening to the politician's answers. Not listening looks bad on camera (it looks as if you are not interested and then the viewers tend to get bored too).

Ask simple open ended questions. If the politician knows her subject she will be able to give interesting answers.

Avoid questions that simply ask 'How do you feel about...?' You will often get a one or two word answer.

As a general rule avoid double questions 'Why isn't there enough food in your village and what are you going to do about it?' The politician has too much to say in one go.

Avoid really long complicated questions, every one gets bored and the politician and viewer will forget what you are really asking.

Avoid asking too many obvious questions. For example, 'Would you like more food in your community?'

Avoid questions which simply have the answer 'yes' or 'no'.

Ask questions in a logical order. For example, do not ask the politician what she is going to do about a problem before finding out what the problem is.

Confident children can ask supplementary questions that are based on what the politician has just said. For example, an answer that states that there is a food shortage because there has not been any rain for a year could be followed up by a supplementary question that asks, 'How do you water the crops you usually grow?'.

In the example above, supplementary questions would be very useful after the politician has explained his policy to deal with the food shortage. For example, if she says, 'We are going to buy our food from another community.' The reporter could ask, 'Where are you going to get the money from?' In this way, the interview starts to become more like a conversation.

Children can be taught and can practise these techniques. In this project, there is no need to edit the video clips. Ask the children to run through the interview in one shot. They can practise off camera. It is also fun to see all the mistakes and stumbles (in a supportive environment) and children will soon learn how to improve how they talk on camera. Finish the project by showing the class a variety of real television news items that include interviews and ask children to comment.

Contemporary art

In the last quarter of the twentieth century, contemporary artists made more and more art about issues. Many young artists moved away from an art for art's sake philosophy that seemed to be characteristic of movements such as abstract expressionism. For example, in the 1970s, in the UK, almost all art students in the major art schools produced abstract work that celebrated the sensibilities of materials and formal values such as space, colour and surface. The meaning of this work was often considered beyond the remit of words to explain. However, by the late 1990s it was no longer fashionable to make paintings and sculptures based on formal or aesthetic values alone. Art had to mean something tangible and deal with real issues. In Britain, a pioneer of this way of working was Damien Hirst. He, along with other 'Brit Pack' artists, drove a movement forward that gained institutional acceptance. For example, The Turner Prize, organised at Tate Britain, has become an annual celebration of this kind of contemporary British art that receives considerable news coverage and promotes a great deal of debate.

Organising projects for the classroom that are inspired by contemporary art is a real option for teachers. Far from being difficult, this art is often readily accepted by children who are not prejudiced against its apparent oddness. Children see what there is to see and will talk about contemporary art in a straightforward way. Clearly, the content of some contemporary art is not suitable for children in school. Other artists have such a minimal approach to expressing ideas that teachers will not get enough purchase from the art to generate momentum for work in class. However, the majority of contemporary art is accessible and useful. To illustrate the potential visit the web pages devoted to the Turner Prize at www.tate.org.uk. There is a section devoted to the history of the prize and, for each year from 1984, a list of the artists short-listed each year. There is a brief description of the main ideas behind each artist's work and links about how to find out more. Although on-line resources will change over time, there will always be ways of researching contemporary art. How can ideas expressed through contemporary art inspire original thinking about planning art in the primary classroom? Teachers may not wish to show children the examples described below. The intention is to use the artists' ideas to

suggest fresh directions for planning the content of art in school. Here are three examples of families of ideas prompted by considering Turner Prize artists.

Kutlug Ataman uses video to make his art. He was short-listed for the Turner Prize in 2004. Ataman believes that, 'Identity is not something that you possess, but something that you wear'. People adapt or change their identity in response to life pressures, fears, dreams and beliefs. His videos show people telling stories about themselves and their lives that may not necessarily be true, but which make them feel important or different.

Look back at page 76 about identity and at page 46 about telling a story to video. Children could invent an imaginary story about themselves that will make everyone see them in a different way. For example, something they dream of being or something that they imagine happened to them in the past. The stories are not real, but children could try to tell their imaginary stories to the camera as though they really believe they are true. What other ways could children change their identity? For example, children could work onto digital photographs of themselves (enlarge them on the photocopier to A3) or they might wear costume or paint their faces (look back at page 65).

In 2004, another one of the artists short-listed was Yinka Shonibare; he was born in London but moved to Lagos when he was three years old. Yinka's work deliberately mixes visual cultural references. For example, he takes a painting of a wealthy girl on a swing from 18th century France by Fragonard. He makes a life size sculpture of a girl on a swing, which echoes the painting. However, he changes the fabric of the girls dress to a fantastic looking African cloth. He has removed her head so she is robbed of her personal identity. We are jarred by the frivolity of the wealthy aristocracy in 18th century France placed together with references to Africa that bring to mind ideas about poverty and exploitation by the West. In a paradox, that confirms how clichéd our ideas often are, Yinka is also suggesting that African visual culture is full of life, just as the girl on Fragonard's swing!

Look back at page 70 and ideas about introducing children to different cultures. This is best done after they have had experience of creating their own imaginary cultures as explained in Part 1 of this book. Pick a distinctive African culture to explore with children. How could children explore contrasts between the wealthy West and the poor in Africa, whilst at the same time celebrating the richness of

visual art and design from Africa? Shonibare uses ideas of incongruity. Teachers can use the same approach. For example, how would it look if skyscrapers surrounded an African village? What if a street of suburban British houses were painted with African colours and designs? How about repainting an expensive car with the same African colours and designs? Alongside a still life of wonderfully coloured fruit, could children paint a still life showing what the poorest African children would eat in a day?

Anya Gallaccio was short-listed in 2003. Anya often uses materials that change over a period of time. For example, flowers, chocolate and grass. The artist might hang hundreds of flowers in a gallery window. At first, they look fresh, full of life and colour. As time passes, the flowers dry and even decay and we are made aware of the sensitivity of the natural world to time. In another installation, Gallachio places a large floral rug deep in woodland. As time passes the rug, with its manufactured images and repeated patterns derived from nature, disappears back into the woodland floor as plants and natural debris gradually cover the woven surface.

How could children explore change in natural materials? Could they set up an installation of various substances that are going change over time? For example, fruit that will rot, flowers that will dry out, colours that will fade, grass and plants that will grow, ice that will melt? What happens if an object is placed on a patch of ground, which remains untouched over the summer term? How does the object change? How does the environment it is in change? How could children record these changes? In what other ways could children explore change over time? How about, growth, metamorphosis, decay, erosion, weather, moods? A project could be designed around the concept of change over time which itself is presented in the form of a sequence of photographs, drawings, video or an art installation.

3.3 Finding out about the environment

Many potential projects could be categorised under the banner of the environment. After all, the children's environment includes the classroom, home, inside the school, outside the school, the town, city or village they live in, the landscape, the cityscape, ponds, playgrounds and gardens. One could also include topics like mini beasts, houses and homes, and natural and made materials.

Many art schemes of work have units of work that include the concept of investigating. For example, this might include projects that feature sketchbooks, observational drawing, recording and collecting. There is a wealth of good advice about these kinds of teaching strategies available from publications and the Internet.

Often, the idea is that children experience, observe, record and collect visual ideas about the environment, let's say by visiting a park near the school. They are then taught a skill or technique, for example, observational drawing or colour-mixing in paint. This leads to a finished piece of work. Projects such this are enhanced and sometimes led by showing children relevant examples of work by adult artists.

However, if you are reading this after having explored other sections of this book, you will have found that the inspiration for the art children make comes from strategies that give them control of the ideas and the meanings. These are then expressed in many different forms through art in its broadest sense. To recap, this is intended to motivate children and leave them in creative control, whilst still within a precinct of ideas established by the teacher who will have various educational and curriculum objectives in mind. The whole process echoes the way cultures, large and small, develop.

In this section, we are going to look at how some of the excellent and well-established teaching practices about investigating the environment can be enhanced and incorporated into the kinds of projects found in this book. »151

Starting with key ideas

Teachers can use a single key idea to act as a fulcrum and catalyst for planning projects. The approach of starting with a 'Key Idea' has been pioneered in the USA as part of a project called Transforming Education Through the Arts Challenge (TETAC). This section of the book has been inspired by TETAC but is an adaptation of it. Key ideas, together with associated 'essential questions', help children begin a process of enquiry. More usefully, they help teachers plan a structure for a creative project that supports children through a questioning and investigative process that helps them to work meaningfully. This motivates them. Key ideas are characterised by complexity, ambiguity, contradiction, paradox, and multiple perspectives. The point is that a key idea is open, not closed. They can also combine elements of both the concrete and abstract in a provocative way. They invite questions rather than suggesting ready answers. Key ideas allow children to ask questions about the world and about themselves, and they call for an understanding of more than one point of view.

The essential questions that usually accompany a key idea help to reveal connections and posibilities. A key idea can be turned into essential questions by re-phrasing it. Essential questions give conceptual direction and invite children to see the bigger picture. The choice of the key idea and essential questions is important. Ideas and questions could be connected with the existing curriculum and, at least in part, they are likely to reflect the knowledge and interests of the teachers, as well as those of the children.

Investigating the environment

A possible key idea is: *people who live in cities need parks*. This can be rephrased in a series of essential questions that will lead the investigative studies and motivate the children's artwork. For example, what is life like in the city? Why do people go to parks? What kinds of things make a park a nice place to visit? What are the problems with parks? What is the park like in our neighbourhood? What would be in an ideal park? Essential questions will help define the key idea for the teacher who can now use these to plan the project. The first step is to introduce the project to children:

During this project we are going to look for ideas that will improve the park. We are going to visit the park to find out what's there. We will make some art that shows what the park is like. You will work out ideas about how to improve the park and design parts of a brand new park. I have spoken to Mr Griffiths, our local councillor. He is taking a great interest in our project and when we have finished the work will come to school to look at your work and hear your ideas.

Now ask children to discuss, brainstorm or mind-map the first three of the essential questions above: What is life like in the city? Why do people go to parks? What kinds of things make a park a nice place to visit? Talk about the ideas the children come up with.

For the next session, organise a visit to the park (or a recreation area) or you could also adapt this project to think about school playgrounds. Plan how the children are going to observe, investigate and record the environment. It is quite likely that one visit is not going to be enough.

Here are some ideas for activities in the park. Divide the children into manageable groups with an adult with each group. First ask children to talk about what they can see in the park, go into as much detail as you feel necessary. Ask the adult or the children themselves to make a word list. Support this by inviting children to use a digital camera to record the different ideas mentioned in the first activity. Each group will have a collection of digital images and words.

Next try an activity that will involve visual investigation; tried and tested activities centred on the visual elements might be useful here. For example, children could record shapes, colours and textures. They might make observational drawings of the park using drawing boards and A2 paper. An activity that helps children draw space (background, middle ground and foreground) could work well. You could make further use of the digital camera. For example, children could make rubbings of the different textures associated with different materials used in the park, but why not

also take close up photographs of the textures? The photographs will look quite abstract, but could work well when displayed with all the other information. **»151**

Back in school, the class could make a piece of art about the park. For example, paintings could be made based on the drawings and photographs. These could celebrate something beautiful about the park, the flowers, the lake, and the trees. Children could draw an illustrated and annotated map of the park showing everything they discovered about it. Even without additional artwork, children will now be ready to think about more essential questions back in class. What is the park like in our neighbourhood? What are the problems with parks? What would be in an ideal park? The second question might be best rephrased as, 'What are the problems with our park'?

To help children explore ideas at a deeper level again, the teacher might prepare a set of sub-questions to each of the essential questions in the last paragraph. For example, thinking about 'What are the problems with parks?' could lead to asking:

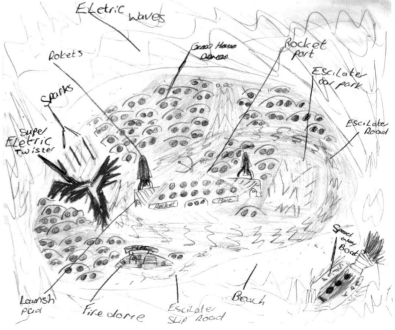

Do people always feel safe in parks? Why not?
What kind of work is needed to keep a park
looking good?
Who should pay for the park?
What do people like to do when they visit the park?
Do children and adults like the same things in
the park?
Who is the park for?
How could the park look better?

Now children will be ready to design their ideal park. There may be different sections to this new park, which are tackled by different groups. They may need to visit the park again to look at their own brief in detail. For example, one group could look at the play area for young children, another at a play area for older kids; a group could look at the layout of the paths, flower beds and shrubs; there could be better sporting facilities in the park. Is there water in the ideal park, a water play feature, a pond, or a lake? Thinking about ponds, what about the wildlife? One group could design ideas for helping birds, mammals and fish enjoy the park too!

Remind the children if someone like a councillor or a landscape architect is coming to visit. This may be particularly significant if this project follows one linked to politics (see page 126). Motivation is a powerful tool in promoting creativity. Children will make more effort if they see that their work has some significance outside the classroom and the usual curriculum.

Children will need to be able to work out ideas in rough using quick drawings and notes. Words can be an important aid to firming up ideas and a help to the less visually gifted. Ask children to make a finished drawing of one or more of their final ideas. The children could make models of equipment for play. They could paint or draw an imaginary view of the park showing all the improvements, or simply an imaginative vision of flowers, trees and animals. Perhaps they could make an imaginary drawing or painting of a wildlife area, which shows some of the creatures that could be attracted to the park. »151

Finally, they need to come together to present their ideas for an ideal park. This may be in the form of an exhibition, a class book, and a presentation. Look back at pages 46 and 131 for ideas about using reporting and presenting techniques for television. Children will work hard on their presentation if they know a special visitor is coming into school.

Here are some more ideas about projects that focus on the environment that use a 'key idea' approach to start the planning process. You could design a teaching structure similar to the park project above.

This project theme is linked to houses and homes. Key Idea: *Every one needs a home*. Supplementary questions: What different kinds of homes are there? What would it be like if you didn't have a home? What kinds of things are there in a home? What do homes look like from the outside? What makes a good home? What would your dream home be like? This project could be linked to animal homes and to the work on imaginary people (page 77). The work could be developed into architecture (see page 120).

Key Idea: *Streets are busy places*. This project is going to explore an urban street and everything that makes up street life. Supplementary questions: Why do people use the street? What happens on the street? What happens in the buildings along the street? What can you see? What can you find? How could the street be made better? What will a street of the future look like? This project offers a great opportunity to look at street culture.

Key idea: *We all make rubbish!* This project is linked to ideas about recycling. Supplementary questions: Why is there rubbish? How much rubbish is there? Who makes rubbish? What happens to rubbish? What do you think should happen to rubbish? Can we do anything useful with rubbish? This project could easily move towards junk modelling and collage.

Key idea: *People like nature*. Supplementary questions: Who lives in the countryside? What do people who live in the country do for a living and recreation? What are the best things about the countryside? What can you find when you look at a landscape? What can you find when you walk through a landscape? Why do people like nature? What is beauty? This project can offer a way into understanding more about artists who use landscape as a central theme of their work.

Old toys and digital photography

Here is an example of a project that links with some of the themes running through Part 3. Art can be made from junk or from discarded or unwanted objects. In a slightly different form, the project could feature ideas about recycling or objects found in the environment. This work also links with ideas about contemporary art and in particular the possibility of installations. The transformation or metamorphosis of objects is a well-established theme in secondary school art education.

Ask each child to bring in an old and unwanted toy. Before the practical work starts, children could get together in groups to work with ideas. Look back at page 98 and the advice about making up a dream story. Use the toys in the same way as the objects to help prompt a narrative. Children who have been working on projects in other parts of this book may already be in quite well-established imaginary communities. In this case, the narratives will be linked to the imaginary cultures they may already be creating. Perhaps the toy could have magical powers or is a symbol for something important in an imaginary community. The same project structure could work with any significant objects.

Explain the sequence of events. First they are going to have to think about a photo set in which the toys are going to be arranged for a photograph. You could introduce the idea of 'still life' here. Provide different choices for the set. Old boxes, fabrics, coloured papers might be useful but really anything is possible. Why not use fake grass, real turf, twigs, plants, photographs and posters to make backgrounds

creating illusions of somewhere different. Let the children suggest both what to use and where to find it. A choice of coloured fabrics can be hung behind a set to completely hide the usual classroom walls.

Next children are going to paint their toy. This transforms it, at least in colour. The best way is to buy quick drying acrylic spray paint, children could choose between several colours. The big problem here is that an adult will have to do the spraying, these paints are too noxious to be used in school – check the relevant health and safety advice. The advantage is that you can really cover the entire toy quickly and easily. Children could watch from a distance! However, children could paint their own toys with a ready-mix paint or even household emulsion. It is a good idea to coat the whole toy in a 50:50 mix of PVA and water. This will seal the surface and help the ready-mix paint to adhere to smooth plastics and metal. This will delay things a bit, as some of the toys could take quite a time to dry. Tell the children not to expect to cover every part of the toy. The most problematic toys are furry animals. You could exclude them because they are difficult to paint, or persevere and treat them in the same way as everything else even if they look a bit odd. Alternatively, find another way to transform them. What would the children like to do?

How is each group of children going to arrange the toys in the photo set? What are the different possibilities? What props could they use? Is there a story about how the toys are arranged or is it best simply to try out different ideas until something just looks right? Children could try out various possibilities.

They will need support to get the best photograph. Will the camera attach to a tripod? Tripods are useful because they stabilise and slow down the whole process and not just in the sense of hands shaking! There are several controls. For example, up and down, side to side and tilt. Children can see how these work and learn to tighten them when they have the right position. A helpful adult on hand will be a boon with younger children. Does the camera have a zoom lens? If so, children can consider whether they want to zoom in to details of their arrangement. It is best for them compose their shot on the standard lens setting first. For many cameras this is all the children will need to think about although there may be relevant settings for different lighting conditions.

How is the still life going to be lit? Most cameras have built in flashes but it can be more fun to turn the flash off and use directional lights. These can create shadows. Sunlight is useful too. Children can adjust two or three light sources such as the light from an overhead projector or slide projector to try to get a lighting effect that looks good. If the camera is sophisticated enough to operate well in low light conditions they could try other forms of light such as desk lamps, torches, lamps and fairy lights. The tripod is probably essential if you turn off the flash and you are working indoors. Having said that, the project works fine even if the children simply illuminate the still life with the flash.

Finally, children need to compose the shot. They will need to position the camera, adjust the height of the tripod and think about what they want inside and outside the frame. Many digital cameras will connect directly to a laptop and children will be able to see their photographs on the screen almost right away. This is very helpful as they can make the subtle changes to improve the product. Discarded shots can be deleted. Each child in the group can have a chance to find their best shot and best arrangement inside the set bearing in mind all the variables noted above. Treat the finished photographs as art objects.

For a completely different idea read through the text again, only this time imagine that the children stake out a rectangle on the grass, or mark out a rectangle in chalk on the playground. Each toy is placed in regimented fashion as close as possible one to another until the rectangle is full. A photograph is taken. The activity is repeated several times with the children choosing how to set up the area in which to photograph the toys. The finished artwork is a series of digital photographs that show the extraordinary variety of colour, form, shape and texture of toys. This project could be adapted to deal with environmental concerns. Replace the idea of toys with plastic packaging from home that would normally be thrown away. Contrast this with other materials such as glass and then with natural materials.

Ask children to brainstorm how they could enhance the meaning of the installations by adding sound or video. For example, they could create a chant linked to the subject of the installation (see page 122). This could be recorded and played back as viewers see the final work. They could create short animated videos with toys (look back at page 48). These moving images could be displayed on a screen in the toy installation. Perhaps the effect would be to suggest

that toys, far from being lifeless, have characters and lives of their own. Thinking back to the wall of family images, perhaps each child could record a story that they create about a member of their family. This could be completely imaginary or real. The children tell their stories to video (see page 46) these are played back as part of the installation.

If you have read as far as here, you will realise that ideas are almost limitless. Look at installations by contemporary artists to inspire ideas. Think about ways children can take control of the meaning. Use the installations as a way of stimulating debate and interest in issues. Mix and match techniques. Painting can go with story telling, music with photography, drawing with writing, sculpture with video.

Art for the community

In this section, we have already seen how the environment theme offers a wealth of meaningful contexts for children's art. For this project, children are invited to create art in a community context. But what is meant by community? Limiting ourselves to ideas about local communities, it can simply mean a group of people living in a particular local area, or in a residential district. More specifically, it could be a group of people having ethnic, cultural or religious characteristics in common (for example, the Bengali community in East London). There are buildings and places in communities where people come together for various purposes. These include schools, hospitals, places of worship, community centres, sports halls, railway and bus stations, shopping areas, parks, walking and cycling paths and more besides. Can children create ideas and plans for artwork specifically for one or more of these kinds of places? Look forward to the next section for more specific ideas about site-specific sculpture. This project is going to consider opportunities for two-dimensional art.

It is difficult to find a school in the United Kingdom that has not benefited in some form from working with artists in the recent past. Artists can bring new ideas and energy. They can help teachers and children lift themselves out of humdrum school art styles, towards something exciting and unexpected. Artists can bring specialist skills, tools and equipment. They are used to working on larger scales than children normally experience. All in all, working with artists can be refreshingly creative. There are many artist-in-school projects in which artists more or less control the products, inviting some contribution from children. Children can create ideas that artists can incorporate into the work, or they can help the artists make the finished artwork. More negatively, children can sometimes appear to be simply recreating a 'look' or an aesthetic appreciated only by the artist. Children can be enthused and excited to do this but have a very limited understanding or control over the meaning of the activity. In contrast, this project explores how children can set the agenda for the artist (or themselves if no artist is available).

Children can work in groups or as individuals. Group work means more sharing of ideas and abilities. One approach is to create ideas in groups but follow through design work as individuals. The project divides into five sections: identifying a suitable context for the artwork; planning the project; developing and presenting a design; producing an end product; showing and evaluating the final outcomes. Artists could be involved in each stage of this process, which is designed to echo how they would approach a community commission themselves. Teachers may want to establish in advance the media to be used, although this may be dictated by the particular skills of any artist involved. However, this project will work well if the children simply make designs for the eventual piece of community art, even if they are unable to see these ideas fully realised.

Children could start by looking at a map of the local community or they could make an exploratory walk. Children or teachers could prepare a series of digital photographs or a video to show children some of the significant places in their community. Can they identify public places where people might enjoy an artwork? Here are some ideas: an old people's home; a hospital; a doctor's surgery; a shopping centre; a sports hall; a nursery school; a place of worship. Ask children to talk about who uses these kinds of places and why a work of art might be a good or bad idea.

The next step is to select suitable venues and see if it is possible to organise a visit. Children will need to meet someone in charge and, if possible, some of the users of the venue. If this is difficult, a teacher (or the artist) could use video to interview a manager and look at a potential place for the artwork. Look back at page 131 for ideas about interview techniques and how to prepare questions. Children could be involved in choosing a site. This is realistic only if they are designing an imaginary artwork that will probably never be made. If the project involves real art, then adults will have to take the final decision.

The children will need digital photographs of the site. These can be printed on A4 paper in black and white. Use a photocopier to make enlargements to A3. For example, the team may have identified a wall in a doctor's surgery. Patients waiting to see the doctor would enjoy a work of art. What could be the subject of the artwork and how would it be made?

One possibility is to leave each group in the class to decide themselves. Another is to suggest that as the school has a ceramicist-in-residence (just as an example) so the final piece will be a ceramic tiled mural. Alternatively, teachers may wish to direct children towards a process that is pre-planned as part of a scheme of work. For example, painting, weaving, printing, work with textiles and so forth.

If the opportunity exists for representational subject matter, then teachers can link this project to almost any part of this book. To mention a few ideas: the environment; architecture; identity; imaginary islands; imaginary animals; imaginary machines; patterns; religious motifs and abstraction. The final choice of subject could well be something discussed with the client. Perhaps children could shortlist two or three and the client can choose? Children will be very motivated if they know someone from outside the school (the director of a health care trust for example) is going to listen to their ideas and look at the work.

Children's ideas for the design could come after following the kinds of projects described throughout the book. However, they will need to be given (or work out for themselves), the size and shape of the finished piece. This can be drawn onto a print out of a digital photograph of the place where the prospective artwork is going to be sited. The format of the rectangle, if it is a rectangle, can then be kept constant as they work out their ideas, say, five units high by nine wide. There are many different ways groups and individual children can either share or work individually on the design. For example, in

the case of the ceramic mural already mentioned, children could each design one tile. The role of a visiting artist can now be examined as, perhaps, the children suggest ideas to the artist who draws up various possibilities. Children may go on to help with or even make the eventual full size artwork. However, if this is impossible, the project can be concluded as children make smaller versions. These can be digitally photographed, cropped and pasted onto an image of the actual site.

Some community art projects result in competitions. Children could prepare a visual, written and oral presentation about their ideas. Managers, residents, patients, parents, indeed anyone who uses or visits the chosen site could be involved in listening and choosing a winning design. Their comments and the children own thoughts will form part of the evaluation. Teachers will have already noticed that links to curriculum ideas about citizenship can play an important role in this project.

Beastie Bench, Gwen Heaney, Cardiff Bay

Site specific sculpture

One art form often seen around our towns and cities is sculpture. Site-specific sculpture is made for a particular location. Often these works commemorate an event (a war, the coronation); a person (for example, think about the many historical statues in town centres) or have been made to enhance a new development. You can find site specific sculptures on roundabouts, in marinas, shopping centres or on cycle trails. Nowadays, many new commissions are in the form of a competition. The artist works with the opportunities and constraints of the site and the subject to design and make a sculpture. At the very least, artists are asked to draw up plans and proposals, these are then short-listed and the individual artists interviewed before a final choice is made. Costs and budget restrictions play a vital part, as does the selection of appropriate materials for both safety issues and climate. The community is sometimes involved in helping to set a brief for the artist and in selecting the final piece. For example, around the Cardiff Bay development in South Wales, amongst a plethora of commissioned art works, there are benches to sit on, a low wall inscribed with fossil like motifs and text, a memorial to merchant seamen and gates and a fence for a primary school. Arts agencies often help liaise between the client and the artist, helping to establish the brief, draw up contracts and oversee the work.

Teachers will be able to find information about commissioned site-specific art works by contacting an arts agency in their area. For example, in England, at the time of writing, there are many links available at www.artscouncil.org.uk. Information is also available on-line for Scotland, Northern Island and Wales. How can this wealth of ideas, imagery and information help children in the classroom?

First, the critical question must be, 'Why is the artwork being made? Who and what is it for?' Why not look back through the various parts of this book for ideas? Visit the previous page for ideas about linking to real life communities. Link the whole project with the creation of imaginary communities, religions and political issues found in Parts 1 and 3.

One strategy would be to design a competition for the children to design an artwork for a specific site in or near the school. The teacher will draw up rules and instruct the children on how to present their ideas. Many of the strategies that have already been described in this book can be used to create designs and teachers can search for more ideas about drawing, collage, working in clay and construction, all of which may prove useful. Here iare some guidelines that could be adapted for the children to follow: **»151**

- *The finished artwork is especially made for the site. You will visit the site to take photographs, make drawings and make notes about what the site is like and what you can see, smell, touch and hear.*

- *The artwork is for the people who visit the site. It should be interesting. Who visits the site? Why do they come? What kind of art would they like to see? You will need to decide exactly where the artwork will be placed. Does it have a front and back? Can people move around it?*
- *The artwork will have to be safe.*
- *You are free to decide what kind of artwork will look the best.*
- *The finished artwork will need to be made of suitable materials. Think about the weather, how it will be fixed down, does the artwork need protecting in some way?*

Teachers could help children by providing a list of ideas about the kinds of artworks that they could consider designing:

- *Carved stone, carved wood, metal sculpture, sculpture made on the ground with earth or concrete, wind powered works, artworks that use water, artworks that use sound, artworks that people can use or play with, artworks that use light.*

Children could visit a number of site specific artworks to get ideas, or, at the very least they could look at some digital images, many of which can be found on the internet through web sites such as www.artscouncil.org.uk. After visiting the proposed site, taking photographs and making visual and written notes children could:

- *Draw different ideas for your artwork, write notes about what it will look like and what it is made of. Find a way to show its size.*
- *Use this large black and white print out of a digital photograph of the site to test out how your idea might look in place. You can draw your idea onto the image. Or, photocopy your design, reduce it or enlarge it on the photocopier until it is the right size and then collage it onto the black and white image of the site. You can add extra colour and text afterwards.*
- *Could you make a model (a maquette) of your best ideas? What materials would you need. Remember maquettes are only roughs for the finished article so you can use anything that will help show what the finished work might be like.*
- *You could work in small groups or individually. Remember many artists work in small teams and help each other on projects.*
- *Make a final list of all the tools and materials you think you would need to make the real artwork. Would you need any special help? For example, would you need a metalworker, a builder, an engineer, an electrician, a plumber, a crane driver, a lorry driver or anyone else with special skills?*
- *Make a list of any problems you think you might have if you tried to make the artwork. Make a separate list of any problems other people might think of if they saw the finished artwork on the site.*

To finish the project, children could prepare a presentation about their ideas. Look back at page 46. Presenting to camera will motivate children. This kind of work would link up well with an artist in school project. Some of the processes of idea generation could feed into the artist's own work or the artist could help children realise their ideas. If you work with younger children, and the detail of the above project seems too sophisticated, try the following abbreviated approach:

- Find examples of different kinds of sculptures in public places to show children.
- Talk about what they can see.
- Visit a place where children could think about making an artwork.
- What kind of thing would the people who use the place like to see? Devise a strategy to help children think about who visits the site and what kinds of artworks they might enjoy.

- Use A3 black and white printouts of the site and ask children to draw ideas for the artwork onto the copies. They should use strong graphic media and colour. Use image software or a tone control on the copier to make the printouts paler, so that the children's drawings stand out.
- Children could work in groups to make ideas for the artwork. For example, look for advice about construction and working in clay. »151

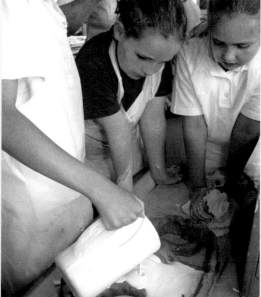

End Piece

Imaginary places

In Part 1, children were invited to create and inhabit communities on an imaginary island. There were also suggestions about imaginary worlds and imaginary cities. There are other possibilities. One way to explore ideas is to look at our real world culture for clues. Literature, film and television offer a plethora of examples of imaginary places. Here are some examples.

The recent US science fiction series 'Battle Star Galactica' sees the human race reduced to a few tens of thousands of people surviving in a fleet of assorted spacecraft. There is no planet, country or city – no geographical place – and yet politics and culture continue, even flourish. If each group of children in the class were in one of the fleet of spacecraft, how would they cooperate, what differences would emerge? How could they express through the arts their experiences of travelling through space?

The reality TV phenomenon has created its own form of imaginary place. For example, the 'Big Brother' house is real enough, but the situation of the inhabitants and what they do is far from everyday. Here, the circumstances of the house are, in a way, imaginary. Holiday swap shows are another example of how real people, in this case families, can experience a series of unusual circumstances that they would never have imagined. The challenge for the classroom is to create a set of circumstances that children could imagine experiencing as a group. What happens? How could each group express the many ideas that are inevitably generated? Perhaps television itself is the cue. Could children invent and then make their own TV presentation, even a whole show? There are some examples of the potential of working with digital video in the book.

For a more classical example, Jonathan Swift's protagonist, Lemuel Gulliver, visited some very strange places. Perhaps the class could consider the experiences of a single character who passes through extraordinary experiences created by the children themselves. Alternatively, perhaps they could imagine living in the different cultures and communities created by Swift. What art, songs, dances and stories would the Lilliputians create?

Utopias and dystopias

Utopias and dystopias are imaginary places of a special kind. Utopia derives its meaning from the Greek words *outopia*, meaning 'no place' and *eutopia*, meaning 'a place where everything is right.' A utopia in fiction is an imagined place where everything seems perfect; it is a vision of a socially and politically perfect society. There could be economic utopias, political utopias, religious utopias, technological utopias, aesthetic utopias and any combination of these. A dystopia is the opposite of a utopia and these places are often characterised by an authoritarian or totalitarian form of government, which exercises some kind of oppressive social control – think of George Orwell's *1984* or the films *Bladerunner*, *Mad Max* or *Waterworld*.

Ideas about perfect places, or conversely places which in one way or another are as bad as they could possibly be, are powerful catalysts for the imagination. Of course, although utopias and dystopias are extremes, the moral dilemmas, decisions and compromises involved in our real world communities are in part influenced by our perceptions of what is ideally good and what is unremittingly bad. Children, even when quite young, can be inspired by imaginative worlds that bring ethical questions into play. For example, a primary school project undertaken in South Wales took the key idea 'rescuers and helpers can make a difference'. The was a part of the City of Cardiff's response to the Holocaust Memorial Day in January 2006. Teachers were invited to use planning strategies that enabled children to generate the content of the project in the classroom and come to understand more about how individuals are faced by moral choices. A team of artists working with digital media, especially photography, offered their skills and expertise in school to help children realise their ideas.

The philosophers island

Finally, let us return one more time to an imaginary island. Only this time it is a philosopher's island. Children are shipwrecked or survive a plane crash (as in Golding's *Lord of the Flies* or for a contemporary adult version of the same theme, look out for the hit 2005 US TV serial *Lost*). In this project, the children are actually on an imaginary island, although they don't know this yet. What can they find out about the environment? How are they going to survive? What are the most important things to do first? What do they want to do first? As the questions develop, the children create a mental picture of an imaginary place. Clearly, this is much more than just a geographical idea, as they will soon encounter moral issues. Quickly, they will be discussing not just how to survive physically but how they feel emotionally, including ideas such as what and who they miss, who is going to look after them, hope of rescue – but also the excitement of exploring and being in charge. Teachers can use these scenarios to introduce philosophical questions. How do you know you survived the plane crash? Maybe it is all a dream. Are the same things that were right and wrong at home going to be right and wrong here? Whether or not you pursue a philosophical direction, this kind scenario is a powerful motivating force. As the children's ideas unfold, teachers will see numerous opportunities for expression through the arts.

Conclusion

This book has been about imagination, culture and creativity but it has also been about motivation – and not just for children but their teachers too. Rather than teaching art skills and concepts divorced from meaning, our imaginary communities and personalities have been the means to give back control of content to children. Because they create the ideas, rather than absorb ideas created for them by adults, children love this kind of work. It is so much easier to teach children a skill or a technique, or introduce them to more abstract concepts, when they are motivated by ideas they have created and continue to command. This makes teaching, as well as learning, easier and a lot more fun.

The complexities of imaginary cultures echo the complexities of real societies. Politics, belief systems, mythologies, the inner individual, the environment, identity, public events all show how varied primary school art projects can be. The features of creativity described in the introduction, are close to the heart of working in this way. As John Steers observes these include tolerance of ambiguity, playfulness with ideas, materials and processes, teasing and worrying away at a problem, unlikely connections and juxtapositions, self-awareness, the self confidence to take risks and the confidence to be intuitive. Once teachers have planned the structure for the kinds of projects exemplified in this book, children's imaginative responses will lead the work. The imagination of children sustains the imagination of their teachers. Teachers can step back. They do not need to be continually creating imaginative ideas of their own. Again teaching is easier, a lot more fun but also more purposeful.

Building imaginary cultures helps children make meaningful art, but the work also has wider value. In the government document, 'Developing the Global Dimension in the School Curriculum', published by the Department for Education and Skills, in March 2005, schools are invited to consider the broader aims of the curriculum:

The global dimension incorporates the key concepts of global citizenship, conflict resolution, diversity, human rights, interdependence, social justice, sustainable development and values and perceptions. It explores the interconnections between the local and the global. It builds knowledge and understanding, as well as developing skills and attitude.

It seems self-evident that technology and the inevitable globalisation that follows, is creating a very different kind of world for our children. Multi-racial, multi-ethnic and multi-cultural societies are becoming the norm in the West. It is easier to help children respect other cultures and value and understand their own, if they can experience and understand more about how cultures are formed and are expressed.

Nigel Meager
January 2006

>> Appendix

This appendix includes additional information and advice. For example, there is help about teaching specific skills. The web site addresses were correct at the time of publication. However, even if these links change it is usually possible to find the organisations concerned using an Internet search facility.

START
This is a magazine for primary and pre-school teachers of art, craft and design published by NSEAD. Each issue features well-illustrated articles by classroom teachers, art education specialists, artists and gallery educators. The subjects are wide ranging and teachers will find many original and contemporary ideas. There is much in START about working with other cultures and ways of fostering creativity in the classroom. Information about how to subscribe to START and about the NSEAD web site is available at www.nsead.org or by calling 01249 714825.

The units of work on the NSEAD web site
The National Society for Education in Art and Design has over 300 units of work on their web site at www.nsead.org. These can be accessed via a password. Subscribers to START and members of NSEAD gain free access to these on-line projects.

The units of work cover the basic skills and processes. There is content suitable for children from 3 to 15 years old. There are ideas about teaching shape, line, space, form, texture, pattern, colour and tone. There is advice about the processes of painting, printing, collage, using clay, construction, and working with fabrics and drawing. The database is searchable using key words.

Teaching Art at Key Stage 1 and Teaching Art at Key Stage 2
Published by NSEAD in 1993 and 1995 respectively, TAKS1 and TAKS2 were also written by Nigel Meager. The books cover this author's approach to teaching the basic skills and processes. They were written for teachers who are not art specialists. TAKS1 focuses on the visual elements whereas TAKS2 is more about projects with ideas about designing patterns, jungles, landscapes, portraits, figures, buildings, architecture, sculpture and war. Both books contain specific and detailed advice about painting, printing, collage, using clay, construction, and working with fabrics and drawing. While still in print, readers can purchase these books direct from NSEAD by calling 01249 714825 or on-line at www.nsead.org/publications.

When the books are finally out of print, they will be published on-line as e-books at www.nsead.org.

References to the NSEAD web site and TAKS1 and TAKS2 in this appendix
Where the text suggests that teachers may want to look for more specific information about a particular visual concept, process or technique, the readers are referred to this appendix. If the information is available at the NSEAD web site or in TAKS1 or TAKS2, this is noted here. In certain cases where it is particularly helpful to do so, a practical classroom strategy is presented in detail.

Page 34:
Information and links about creativity can be found at the Qualifications and Curriculum Authority web site www.ncaction.org.uk/creativity. There are links to National Advisory Committee on Creative and Cultural Education; The Campaign for Learning; Creative Arts Partnership in Education (CAPE); the Creative Centre Educational Trust; Exciting Minds: Creative Partnerships from the Arts Council of England; and the National Endowment for Science Technology and the Arts. Creative Partnerships has a useful database of projects at www.creative-partnerships.com/projects.

Page 35:
Teachers could combine this motif project with strategies that help children explore the visual element of shape. Look at the chapter on shape in TAKS1 and pages 31-47, 66-70 and 84-89 in TAKS2. Search for shape within the units of work at www.nsead.org.

Page 36:
Look at the chapter on pattern in TAKS1 and pages 31-38 and 81-85 in TAKS2. There are many units of work that link to pattern in the units of work at www.nsead.org.

Page 44: Ideas about drawing comics
Start the session by showing children examples of double page spreads from a range of comics and cartoon books. Talk about what the children can see and make a list with them of what devices the artists have used. For example:

- *How are the pages divided up? Are the shapes of the various different areas regular or irregular?*
- *Do the drawings stay inside the boundaries of the shapes? Has the artist included backgrounds? What are they like?*
- *Is there any writing (text)? If so, where is it placed on the page? What style is used to make the letters?*
- *If there is a lot of action in the cartoon, how do the artists show this?*
- *How would you describe the colour? Is it limited to a few colours? What are they?*
- *Are any parts of the drawings exaggerated? If so how?*
- *Does the cartoon show feelings and emotions? How?*
- *What do you like and what do you dislike about the drawings?*

Point out that nearly all the drawings are delineated with dark lines; the colour is filled in between the lines.

Give children an A3 sheet folded into half making two pages of A4 facing each other. The first task is to plan a layout in rough and the second is to use dark outlines and colours to finish the drawings.

Perhaps children could draw the comics for children in their imaginary island communities. The comics will tell important stories from the community in a way children enjoy. Ask them to use the story strips from the previous activity to help them decide what is going to show on the double page spread. Spare paper might be useful if they want to test out ideas. If children need encouragement, they could imitate the style and layout of the double page spreads they liked.

For rough planning, they should use pencils and erasers to set out the areas or boxes containing each part of the story. They will then need to suggest the arrangement of the key elements of the drawings in each space. Encourage children to draw with faint lines to begin as these are easily rubbed out. They may need rulers. If they want to draw curved borders to the comic book sections, they could find curved and circular objects to use as templates. They will also need to plan where the writing is going, as well as the kind of script they will use. When their two pages are more or less laid out, they should begin to go over their faint outlines with a black pen. This maybe the same pens that they use for writing. They will also need to go over any text that they have included although it is possible that some or all of the writing will be coloured rather than black. They may remember that artists varied the thickness of the black outlines in the comic drawings they discussed. Are they able to imitate this technique? Have they access to black pens of varying thicknesses?

When the double page is completely filled with dark outline drawings, they can add colour. This might be best as a separate activity on a new day. This gives the teacher the opportunity to make photocopies of the A3 sheets. These will be useful as part of the display that illustrates the chosen process. Felt pens are an appropriate media for adding colour. Coloured pencils can be used but they tend to have a softer, less bold looking outcome. Finish the project by talking about the results. Perhaps the drawings could be combined into one class book.

Page 49: Animation software
For example, X!PSTER™ is an easy to use computer animation software package. It is very suitable for creating a stop frame animation. It works with most web cams and digital still or video cameras. Children can use a library of sound effects but can also record audio, sound and voice within the application. There is technical advice including ideas about 'horizontal shooting' and 'down shooting'; the importance of saving work as you go; and links to www.xipster.com for more 'tips and tricks'.

Teachers could also consider using Microsoft PowerPoint. Start by taking a simple sequence of photographs – for example a head turning from side to side. Insert the images into PowerPoint and use the animation options to control the amount of time an image stays on screen. Text and sound can be added. Other software packages include Complete Animator www.iota.co.uk/tca.

For examples of projects that involve animation but also link to external arts agencies, artist in school projects and other kinds of support search for animation at www.creative-partnerships.com/projects

Page 51:
Linking patterns in movement and sound with visual patterns is a powerful way to help young children understand the concept of repeating patterns. The chapter on pattern in TAKS1 covers one possible teaching strategy.

Page 52:
Thanks to Robert Cornelius of Cardiff LEA for his help with this example of how to develop music for the imaginary island communities.

Page 55: Making plates
Here is an example of a project that helps children make their own plates. Introduce children to clay. Look for ideas at www.nsead.org or the chapter on form in TAKS1 and p73-74 in TAKS2. Next, introduce the idea of a hump mould (or its inverse, the slump mould). This is a mould, which is in the shape of a 'hump'. Plates can be made as a slab of clay is placed over a shallow hump. If the 'hump' is more pronounced children can make bowls. A slump mould is when the clay is moulded into a hollow. For hump moulds, think of up turned plastic bowls or large rounded pebbles. Slabs of clay can be layered over the hump, trimmed and formed into an upside down bowl or plate shape. Professional hump moulds are generally made of a substance like plaster that will absorb water, the plaster wicks the water away so the moulded clay form dries quickly before it is lifted away from the mould. Many potters will place a layer of muslin of other material between the mould and the clay to make removing the clay form even easier. You can buy commercially made hump moulds – these are sometimes made of once fired bisque clay.

Look forward to page 151, where there is advice on making moulds in plaster. There is no doubt that if the children can take part in, or at least see, the process of making a plaster mould, they will be better able to grasp the idea of how positive and negative forms are used in three-dimensional art and design. In addition, they will have experienced two distinct processes and learnt two skills – working with plaster and working in clay. Plaster moulds can be used repeatedly, but children can also use plastic or metal bowls. Large smooth pebbles and stones from a beach or river make interesting moulds for plates, dishes and bowls. Because they will not absorb water like plaster, the rocks, metal or plastic objects need to be coated with several layers of paper or a damp cloth to help prevent the clay sticking to the mould as it dries. Imagine how the clay shrinks as it loses water, the form wraps itself tighter onto the upturned hump. This can make it very difficult to get off with out breaking or cracking the form. Tear paper into strips (the tough paper towels commonly used in schools work very well), dampen slightly, and make several layers over the mould, alternating the direction of the strips. Make sure the children do this carefully, pressing the damp paper well onto (or into) the form. The paper strips or cloth will actually leave faint textured impressions in the clay. These can be smoothed away later or simply left as part of the design.

When the mould (or object) is ready, the children should roll out clay into an even slab. The slab is then carefully draped over the surface. Excess clay can be gradually worked in as the clay is moulded over the surface of the mould. Using a needle tool cut an even edge around the bottom of the draped clay, which will become the top edge of the plate. To make a surface for the plate to stand on, children can use a flat tool to gently flatten the very bottom of the plate. Alternatively, make a fat coil of clay into a circle, place it gently on the bottom of the plate, trace around it lightly with a pencil. Remove the coil, scratch the area inside the tracing, add enough water to form slip (water and clay mixed to the texture of paste), scratch the underside of the coil, dampen it, place the coil back on the bottom of the plate, gently press the coil in place, and blend some clay from the inside and outside of the coil into the bottom of the object.

Allow the clay to harden slightly (don't forget if the clay is left too long, it will tend to shrink enough to stick or even to crack), lift the mould and plate together, and turn them over carefully (children may need to help each other with this step), then lift the mould out of the upturned form. Alternatively, lift the plate directly off the mould if it is dry enough not to lose its form. There is no substitute for experience. The length of time you need to leave the clay before taking it off the mould varies according to the amount of clay and the room temperature and humidity. Rather than wait too long it is best to take the clay off the mould as soon as it hardened enough to keep its shape. This will probably be a few hours rather than a few minutes. Why not construct an experiment with the children in advance to check on the rate at which different thicknesses and sizes of clay slabs dry? You could also keep the clay moist over night by spraying with a plant mister and placing the plate inside a plastic bag. Potters sometimes use damp towels over the clay to prevent it drying.

When the plate is off the mould, place it squarely on the coil or flattened base and smooth the rim using a small damp sponge, or a moistened fingertip. Cover the objects and allow to harden overnight. It is best if this is not in a hot dry room because they may dry too quickly and crack. In the morning, or as soon as they are stiff enough to handle, turn all the objects over and cover loosely. Allow to continue to dry slowly. (Turning the plates over helps prevent the rim drying so much faster than the base so that the rim cracks.) One obvious problem is storage space for a large number of plates and bowls.

When the tableware (whether it is a plate, dish or bowl) is completely dry. It can be glazed and fired. There are a number of glaze manufacturers who offer glazes that are safe for use in schools. Earthenware glazes will work particularly well with the terracotta clay. If the children want to see the effect of glazes before they apply their design you could organise a test. The children paint different colours onto small slabs of clay, being careful to score the name or number of the colour onto the reverse of the slab. These are then fired and the class can see the change in colour of the glaze from before and after the firing.

It is true that not many primary school teachers have easy access to a kiln. Nevertheless, the plates can be painted and displayed without firing. The children will have to be very careful. Look out for a simple turntable that pottery suppliers sell. One of these will be useful to avoid handling the objects too much and children could paint their tableware one at a time in a quiet and careful way away from distractions. You can apply acrylic or ready mix paint directly onto the plate but a brighter colour will be achieved if the children apply a diluted (50:50) solution of PVA. This will seal the clay and prevent the colour leaching into the surface. The advice on painting bisque ware will apply to painting this hump (or slump) moulded tableware.

This project is intensely skills based. The focus is on a craft that in different forms has been used to create vessels, containers and tableware of all kinds in all parts of the world. The ideas are described in detail here to illustrate how teachers who wish to include a higher level of skills tuition can do so.

Page 56: Weaving

Why not use the back and front panels from commercial packaging boxes? The material is more robust and can be laminated to produce a usable tablemat for their island community. Simply tape the bottom of the warp threads after weaving, and before laminating, to stop the weft strips falling out (for example, you could use 'iron-on' fabric repair tape).

Plain or tabby weave is the simplest form of weaving where the weft goes over one warp thread and under the next in a regular pattern.

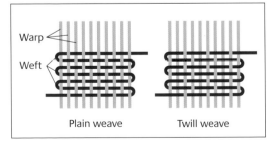

Plain weave   Twill weave

Twill weave produces a diagonal pattern and is used in fabrics like denim. Mark each warp strip in your

template in the sequence 1,2,3,1,2,3,1,2 etc. The pattern is produced by weaving a weft strip under the first number 1 warp, then over the number 2 and 3 warps, under the number 1 warp again, over the numbers 2 and 3, under the number 1 and so on. The next strip goes over the first number 1, under numbers 2 and 3, over number 1 etc. The third strip goes over numbers 1 and 2 and under number 3 and over 1 and 2. The forth strip returns to the first sequence under the first number 1 warp, then over the number 2 and 3 warps etc.

Page 57: Block printing

The best blocks are easy to hold. For example, a block could be a 10cm square of wood about 5cm thick. Buy inexpensive wooden knobs for DIY furniture to screw into the top of the block. On the side used for printing children can glue shapes made out of cardboard or polystyrene printing tiles. These need to be very well glued onto the wood. It is best not to try to print immediately after making the block so that the glue has a chance to dry. The advantage of the polystyrene is that children have no problem in cutting out the shape for themselves with scissors, plus they can score into the surface of the polystyrene shape to create further detail. The cardboard and polystyrene shapes are in relief on the block, adding another layer to the surface of the wood. It is this relief shape that will be printed. If the block is going to used a lot it might be worthwhile sealing the surface with a dilute (50:50) solution of PVA. Cardboard and polystyrene are quite thin so inevitably ink is going to appear on the base ground as the children are inking up the relief shapes. You can ask them to be especially careful, although this may not be a problem as a rough and ready effect is attractive and simply a result of the technique used. If you would like to create long-lasting and hard-wearing printing blocks, a friendly helper with a band saw will need to cut the children's shapes from wood and these can be fixed to the wooden blocks.

Thick cardboard can be used as an alternative to wood to make the block. Grey board is strong and robust enough. The children should cut a handle from a strip of card and glue and tape this to the back of the cardboard base. This will enable them to lift the inky cardboard off the fabric and move it around without touching the dirty side. The relief is made in the same way as above, by gluing card or polystyrene shapes to the surface to form a relief. Children need to be reminded to take special care to make sure their motifs are glued on well. You will need to let the glue dry thoroughly before inking up.

The fabric to be printed can be stretched over a tabletop and held in place with masking tape. Smaller pieces can be held directly onto the table with masking tape. For the very best results, stretch the fabric over a wooden board and tack or staple on the reverse, stretching from the four middle points on each side towards the corners. When the fabric is stretched over a board, it can be moved around easily, leaving tables free for other work. Use white cotton or polyester cotton. A pale coloured background will contrast with the children's designs but a powerfully coloured fabric may be too strong a background for the weaker pigments of some fabric paints.

After you have demonstrated the process, ask the children to go back to their communities to work together to design a pattern that can be made with several blocks. They will need to work out what they are going to repeat, how often and what colour to choose for each motif.

To make the print the children should form a team. The team approach heightens the sense of working together in the imaginary communities already established and jobs can be swapped around. Children learn that they can often achieve a lot more when they work together.

There may be three colours for each of three different blocks. Three children will be each responsible for inking up one colour. Another child is the director in charge of the pattern, making sure the blocks are printed in the right place. A further child is the printer and following directions from the director takes an inked up block from the inkers and prints it onto the fabric. A final child could be responsible for making sure everybody and everything stays clean. A damp sponge and rags are useful to have to hand. Can the children organise themselves to print the fabric?

You can buy fabric paints that can be painted onto the block for printing. Nevertheless, the children can also paint on fabric screen printing ink or use simple water based block printing ink. The block printing ink is more viscous so does not drip and can be rolled onto the block, but most block printing inks are not designed for fabrics. Check with your supplier.

If you are printing on white fabric, the children may choose to add colour to the background after making their prints by using fabric paints.

Page 58: Cold-water paste resist
Mix the paste in proportions of about one and a half cups of flour to one cup of water. Mix gradually using a whisk to get rid of as many lumps as possible. You are aiming for a consistency like double pouring cream. Sieve the mixture to remove any remaining lumps. If you make it the day before store the mixture in the fridge, it may go off. Adding salt delays this a little.

When the children are ready to transfer their designs and ideas to the fabric, pour the paste mixture into a squeeze bottle. You or the children can adjust the rate of flow and thickness of the line by cutting a larger hole in the nozzle. Encourage the children to work fluently but steadily. They will not achieve perfection but, as in everything, if they have a chance to practise first, the results will improve. Several different thicknesses of paste line will add to the final effect. Able children can add quite fine detail.

Page 59: Mono printing
One kind of mono printing involves the application of a water-based printing ink on to a smooth non-absorbent surface such as plastic. Designs are made in the ink. The surface on which the print is to be made is then pressed directly onto the image. Usually two or three prints can be made from the same inky surface before the image becomes faint. Children could draw directly into the ink with their finger, the hard end of a paintbrush or strips of thick card cut to different widths. A second technique involves applying the paper onto the ink before creating the image. Children could then draw onto the paper with a soft blunt pencil, pressing down onto the inky surface beneath the paper. The third

basic idea involves stencils. Shapes can be cut out and placed onto the inky surface before the paper is applied. When the children press down onto the paper, the stencils mask part on the inky surface creating a print. Children can combine all three techniques. Multi coloured prints can be made by letting the print dry each time before adding a second or third layer.

Page 60:
The illustrations show images created by children working with Cloth of Gold as part of a citywide project celebrating Cardiff's centenary as a city. The work was also linked into a wider in-service training initiative, which explored the imaginary island theme. Cloth of Gold is an artist in education company. Find out more by visiting their web site at www.clothofgold.org.uk

Search the units of work at www.nsead.org for more detailed advice about printing in the classroom. This includes how to organise children in teams, how to keep the workspace clean and organised as well as detail of basic printing processes, tools and materials.

Page 67:
There is a wealth of information on-line about puppets and how to make them. For example, search the Internet using the key words 'make' and 'puppet'.

Page 69:
The following is adapted from an article that appeared in START 16 in late 2005. Also, look back at the information on page 5, which, describes a little more about the origins of the ideas. The event took place at the Millennium Centre, Cardiff, in June 2005. The day involved teachers, artists and children. Almost every primary school in Cardiff sent a teacher and head teachers were given an overview of the theory behind the initiative at a conference on the following day. The artists were from different art forms and included dancers, musicians, photographers, visual artists of all kinds, storytellers, poets and designers. From an in-service training perspective, the organisers hoped that teachers would experience a process that could be taken back to the classroom. For example, we hoped teachers would ask themselves questions such as: 'How is culture is meaningful?' and 'How can I help children understand more about art from other cultures?'

The methodology used during the day also highlighted the kinds of conditions needed for creative thinking – particularly, where meaning is created and controlled by children rather than prescribed by adults – be they teachers or artists.

As everyone arrived at the venue, the teachers, artists and children were mixed together. Each group became one of ten imaginary communities on an imaginary island. These communities had characteristics partly allocated by the conference organisers and partly created by teachers, children and the artists during the first hour of mind mapping and brainstorming ideas. For example, the nature of each community would be influenced by its geography – was it located near a volcano, on the coast, in a forest or near a modern city? There were other ways a community's character could be formed – for example, through climate, susceptibility to natural disasters and available technology. From this simple starting point, everyone worked through the day to create a kind of embryonic imaginary culture for his or her community. This included: stories, mythologies, songs, dance, made objects, decorative designs, animation, photography, drawings, prints, jewellery, costumes, and sculptures. There were more esoteric outcomes like beliefs, and the beginnings of politics – how would the community deal with issues?

Each group began work in isolation. They were aware of the other communities but unsure of what they were doing and even exactly where they where. Teachers came together at lunchtime to hear about the background to the ideas and how they could be interpreted in the classroom. These were the kinds of ideas that form the bulk of this book.

The day ended as each community processed through the Millennium Centre, some in costume, others carrying precious objects. They sang and danced, telling the gathering crowd of spectators about the stories, myths or legends that helped give meaning to their imaginary lives.

Page 77:
Search the units of work at www.nsead.org for ideas about drawing people. There is a brief chapter on figure drawing in TAKS2 pp 67-72.

Page 80:
Look at the chapter on portraits in TAKS2 pp 61-66; this focuses on helping children look for shapes, tones, textures and colours. TAKS1 p 68 has advice about helping younger children look for shadows. There are also units of work linked to portraiture at www.nsead.org.

Page 83: Abstraction
This work has been adapted from the kinds of projects that were developed in art schools across the United Kingdom in the 1960s. One of the antecedents of this work is called the 'Developing Process', where students were asked to reinvent their own visual language from scratch. For example, students might be asked to forget everything they ever thought they knew about drawing and revert to a baby-like state where each new mark, line or action was intended to be naïve. They would build something increasingly but loosely meaningful as bit by bit they invented a personal visual language. This language was abstract and sometimes students would be actively discouraged from making representative or realistic drawings as this inevitably meant that they would be using existing conventions, rather than discovering and inventing their own. Whatever your opinion of this way of working and its positive or negative effect on visual art in the last half of the twentieth century, these approaches can have great value for children, who do not have adult preconceptions about the value of abstract versus figurative art.

Page 90:
Colour mixing became one of the key activities as the National Curricula for Art were being developed in the United Kingdom. Teaching children a strategy for mixing colours both developed an awareness of one of the visual elements, colour, and at the same time, children learnt a skill – painting. There is a chapter in TAKS1 on colour and advice on making a painting on p56 of TAKS2. Colour and painting are referenced many times within the units of work at www.nsead.org.

Page 94:
Look online at the Compass database of images at www.thebritishmuseum.ac.uk. You will find a painting by Victor Supurrula Ross. The British Museum comment:

The painting uses acrylic paint on canvas to depict a creation story. It depicts a yarla, a low-growing bush with beautiful pink flowers with potato-like tubers. In one telling of the story, two old men, Jakamarra and Jupurrula, sat down and shook a sacred stone in Yamaparnta, a place near Yuendemu, where the painting was made. The yarla plant grew from the stone, and is believed to be the ancestor of all the plants now found in that place. The concentric circles in the middle of the painting represent the stone, the waving lines the plant growing from it. The two semi-circles are the men. Next to the old men, on the fourth side of the concentric circles, is a food carrier, with some food in it.

Page 95:
There is plenty of advice in this and other publications about talking about art with children. Look at pages 88 and 95. Search the units of work at www.nsead.org for more ideas. Look at p99 and p114 in TAKS 2.

Page 101: Painting
Here is the outline of one technique that will help children make a dream painting.
- Ask the children to use a thin brush (one which has a pointed tip when it is wet). Use white ready-mixed paint and some water.
- Ask the children to copy the lines of the image from their chosen segment onto the painting surface, drawing with the brush and slightly diluted white paint. The paint is very pale but it will show up – just.
- They will need to think about enlarging their drawing and making sure that the images fill the painting just as they did in the much smaller drawing.
- You could explain that these white lines are guidelines. Because they are so pale there should be no worries about redrawing the images if a mistake is made, the mistakes will simply disappear when they add colour.
- For the first layer the children could simply fill in different colours onto their shapes until the painted surface is completely covered. If you use ready-mix paint, you could prepare a whole range

of colours in advance. For example, mixing pots of four different greens, four different yellows, and four different blues and so on. You can add small quantities of white or black to change the colours. This will increase the particularity and complexity of colour. Use round margarine tubs (or similar) with good lids; the paint will keep well if the pots are sealed after use. Of course, the children can mix their own range and this could become an important part of the project. The are many ways of introducing children to colour and colour mixing.

- When the children start painting in colour, encourage them to paint over the white lines so that they are completely hidden. One of the most important disciplines, especially if children are sharing the paint, is to wash and dry their brush each time so that it is clean before they place it again into a pot of colour. They could use a sponge or a rag to dry their brush. An alternative approach is to encourage children to mix colours on a mixing palette.

- Once the first layer is complete and all the white guidelines are covered and the entire painting surface is full of colour, the paint will need to be left to dry properly. This can be an advantage as can children return to their pictures after, say, a day, fresh and re-focused.

- For the second layer why not use oil pastels? These produce strong vibrant colours and enable the children to add more detail. Of course, children could go back and work again using paint.

- If your budget will stretch to a small quantity of better quality acrylic paint, this applied with smaller brushes would help give depth to the colour and add detail. Indeed, children can use almost any media to work on to the first painted layer, try felt pens, soft pastels, biros, coloured crayons, wax crayons and so on. Experienced children will be able to choose the media that pleases them the most and gives the effect that they are looking for.

Display the paintings in an informal way, talk about the images with the children and ask them to describe the part of the dream narrative that inspired them.

Page 103:
The images show children performing as part of a Diversions Dance project in Cardiff. You can find out more about Diversions Dance at www.diversionsdance.co.uk.

Page 105 and 109:
Observational drawing exercises can be daunting if children are not given some guidelines. There is much detailed advice about drawing from observation on the Internet in the units of work at www.nsead.org and in publications. One recommended approach is to use the concepts of key visual elements to help children find a conceptual structure to support them as they work. This could include focusing on shape, line, tone and space for example. Using the visual elements to help children draw is the approach taken in TAKS2 pp 47-54.

Page 105 and 110:
For detailed advice about a strategy to help children use glue and make paper collages search the units of work at www.nsead.org. The chapter on jungles in TAKS2 also has advice about making a collage pp 45-46.

Page 119:
The images are selected from work produced by four Swansea schools that took part in a project with Mission Gallery. The gallery selected four images for printing so that each pupil could have at least five cards to send to family and friends. Mission Gallery also supported the work with old toys and digital photography on page 138. Mission Gallery is supported by Arts Council Wales.

Page 134:
Search the units of work at www.nsead.org for ideas about observational drawing, using sketchbooks and investigating in general. TAKS1 and TAKS2 also contain ideas about drawing and investigating the environment.

Page 136:
Use the drop down menus when searching the units of work at www.nsead.org to help find specific projects that include strategies to help children understand visual concepts such as space, tone, colour, texture, form, pattern, line and shape. These concepts form the chapter headings of TAKS1.

Page 137:
See note for page 100 above for one technique children could use to make a painting. Turn to page 111 in the main body of text to find ideas about construction.

Page 142:
Look for advice about drawing, collage, working in clay and construction within the units of work at www.nsead.org.

Page 143: Plaster casts
Many sculptures in public places are castings, oftenmade of bronze because it weathers well. To understand more about the processes involved children could explore making plaster casts. Using plaster to create casts and moulds is a fundamental sculptural technique that can sit alongside modelling and construction as a potential classroom activity. Casting and using moulds is part of the process used to make many historical sculptures that children can see in museums and in public spaces in the community.

Look back at the possibilities for investigating the environment on page 136 as a starting point for this project. Children could begin by collecting objects that interest them from the outdoors, like twigs, shells, flowers, clean rubbish and junk. Look at page 138; old toys could make an exciting subject to motivate children to learn this skill. Children will need a wooden or cardboard surface for this first activity. Detailed advice about helping children learn about using clay can be found in the units of work at www.nsead.org.

Take some modelling clay and make a ball. Flatten it out on a flat surface, rolling pins are good to use. If the object you want to cast is thick, and you are going to press it in deeply, then leave the clay thick. Next, take your object and press it firmly but gently into the clay. But, be careful not to mark the clay with your fingers, and don't press the object in so deeply that it is difficult to remove. You may need to practise a few times. Gently remove your object so that it leaves an imprint in the clay. You can use toothpicks to gently loosen it from the clay.

Next, bend a strip of cardboard into a ring that will fit around the clay imprint, and tape it with masking tape. Press the bottom edges of the cardboard into the clay, forming a wall around it. You can also tape the ring of card to the board.

You may notice there is a big cardboard box on the work surface. One is part cut away so that you can reach inside it. You are going to both mix the plaster and pour it inside the box. This to stop plaster dust and dirt getting into the classroom. You should wear these disposable gloves or cover your hands with a thin layer of Vaseline. This will stop the plaster sticking to your hands.

To mix the plaster fill this container one third full of water. The container has a lip for pouring. Then take a handful of plaster and sprinkle it slowly onto the water. Then repeat the process again and again until you can see a little hill of plaster appearing on the surface of the water. It may take more plaster than you think. Don't rush. It is done like this to stop air bubbles getting into the plaster mix. When you see the plaster hill peeping above the surface of the water give the container a very gentle stir two or three times with the stick. Remember, it takes longer than you think before the you can see the top of the plaster hill above the water. After stirring, leave it for a minute. Now you can gently pour the plaster into your mould. Do it right away or the plaster will set. If you still have enough plaster you can pour another mould from your group.

Once the plaster is set, remove the tape from the cardboard ring and carefully peel the cardboard away from the plaster cast. When it's completely dry, pull away the clay. You may need to use tooth picks to get all the clay out of little holes and cracks. Work slowly and gently. It is a bit like an archaeologist cleaning an ancient treasure! You can then wash the cast carefully.

The casts can be painted or left as they are. They will make an excellent record of items collected as part of an environmental exploration.

The next method is more direct. Children can take casts of textures and materials applying plaster straight onto the surface. This can work very well with interestingly formed or patterned junk. Coat the object to be cast with a very thin layer of Vaseline, which can be applied with a paintbrush. You will not be able to coat anything very fragile. The Vaseline acts as a barrier. This is particularly important for materials that can absorb water. Cut lengths of scrim. Modern scrim is made of plastic and less pliable than the older hessian scrim, but both can be used. You can buy this from builders merchants. Mix the plaster in the same way as above in the cut away cardboard box. Using the fingers, begin by carefully dripping plaster onto the surface of the material you are casting. Next, take a length of scrim and dip it into the plaster. Remove it slowly and lay it over the material. Repeat this until you have several layers of scrim and plaster. Children can gently smooth the plaster with their fingers. The shape of the cast is irregular. When the plaster is dry lift or peel it from the material. Children will discover a cast of their texture, piece of scrap, junk or pattern. Footprints, handprints, body, and paw prints can be recorded in this way. Children could make imprints in a tray of dense damp sand. The cast is made directly onto the area to be recorded.

Once they get the idea, they can experiment. One problem is more complicated objects with holes and overhangs will trap the setting plaster making it impossible to remove. If the children enjoy the technique and become competent at mixing and using plaster, staying in control of the process, you could develop the skill further. There is plenty of advice on the Internet about different techniques and possibilities linked to making casts and moulds.

Plaster casting can be used as part of other projects in this book. For example, look back at the section on shrines installations and the significance of objects. Children who create imaginary animals could cast their imaginary tracks. Plaster casts could become part of abstract sculptural constructions or used in photographic sets.

She is scared that wen she gos to the monster school all the (monster) kids (at her) (moor) Socs will smell. and she will forget her bits. her dad sed Bahte a Bihte gos ar the hed teacher!

In Vader

It She live's in a city of monsters were it is a green sky. and Slime that is sticki stick on the flor. She sleeps in a bin and never wash she eat's old metal and drink with watter and old juice of a orange she washs hate ice cream crem. funny and she's

Index

Notes

The National Society for Education in Art and Design is the leading national authority concerned with art, craft and design across all phases of education in the United Kingdom. We offer, for a single subscription, the extensive benefits of membership of a professional association, a learned society and the option of membership of an independent trade union.

The NSEAD provides:

- Immediate access to information to keep you up to date with news, views and current developments in art and design education

- Opportunities to participate in debates about art and design and wider educational issues and to make contact with collegues from all phases of education accross the UK and worldwide

- Recognition by government and governmental agencies – the society is consulted regularly and advises on issues related to the subject and more general matters

- Frequent professional development opportunites through an extensive programme of international, national and regional events

- Publications including newsletters and 3 issues of the International Journal of Art & Design Education each year and the option of subscribing to START magazine for those working in a primary phase

- Access to the NSEAD online mail order specialist book shop

- Efficient professional advice on all aspects of employment in education: legal aid is also available if necessary

- Independence – the NSEAD is not affiliated to any other union or political party

- Insurance cover against theft of personal effects at work

- NSEAD visa card at competitive rates and an express loan service both provided by MBNA

Further information from:

www.nsead.org

NSEAD
The Gatehouse
Corsham Court
Corsham
Wiltshire
SN13 0BZ

T. 01249 714825
F. 01249 716138

www.nsead.org

AN INVITATION TO SUBSCRIBE TO START
THE MAGAZINE FOR PRIMARY AND PRE-SCHOOL TEACHERS OF ART, CRAFT AND DESIGN

Published twice a term by the NSEAD, START is full of ideas and resources to help teachers in the classroom.

A year's subscription to **START**, with each half-termly issue containing 24 full colour A4 pages plus a two-sided A2 poster and supporting website access, costs just £30.

Complete the on-line order form at:

www.nsead.org/publications/start.aspx

to receive the next six issues of **START** with free resources and to receive details of how to get free on-line access to an archive of back issues of **START** and over 300 units of work to help you in your teaching.

'While we are at it, could the school subscribe to START? It seems to be a 'hot pop' in the staff room.'

Caroline Corker
Hampton Junior School

'I am delighted with the new magazine START — full of useful information and ideas.'

Emma Nevill
Teacher

'Thank you for such a great art magazine for teachers.'

Rosi Robinson
Head of Art, Cumnor House School

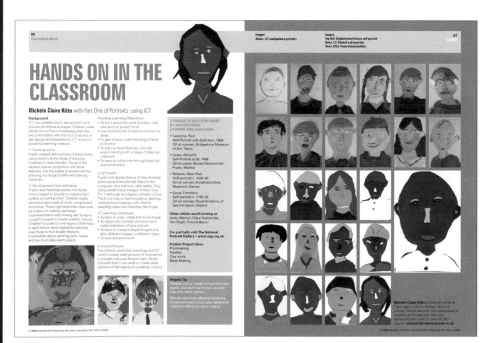